T0323783

Why It's OK
to Be a Gamer

If you enjoy video games as a pastime, you are certainly not alone—billions of people worldwide now play video games. However, you may still find yourself reluctant to tell others this fact about yourself. After all, we are routinely warned that video games have the potential to cause addiction and violence. And when we aren't being warned of their outright harms, we are told we should be doing something better with our time, like going outside, socializing with others, or reading a book. Playing video games is thus often seen at best as a waste of time, and at worst a source of violent tragedy.

Why It's OK to Be a Gamer takes on the pervasive assumption that playing video games is a childish and time-wasting hobby, and a potentially addictive and dangerous one at that. It argues instead that there are many ways in which gaming can help us flourish, for example by: developing genuine friendships and other meaningful relationships with others, helping us cultivate a virtuous personal character, giving us a unique aesthetic experience, providing us with psychological benefits, and just plain helping us relax and enjoy ourselves. Video games are not just for those with no life; on the contrary, they can help contribute to a rich and meaningful life.

Sarah C. Malanowski is Instructor of Philosophy at Florida Atlantic University, USA. She specializes in philosophy of cognitive science and biomedical ethics, and her work has appeared in *Frontiers in Neuroanatomy*, *Synthese*, *Bioethics*, *Journal of Medicine & Philosophy*, and *Neuroethics*. Sarah is also a dedicated *World of Warcraft* player and a casual player of many other video games, and enjoys building cosplays for video game conventions.

Nicholas R. Baima is Associate Professor of Philosophy at Harriet L. Wilkes Honors College, Florida Atlantic University, USA. He specializes in ancient philosophy and ethical theory, as well as *Destiny 2*. His work has appeared in journals such as *Ancient Philosophy*, *Phronesis*, *Journal of the History of Philosophy*, *Ethical Theory and Moral Practice*, and *Journal of Value Inquiry*. He is the coauthor, with Tyler Paytas, of *Plato's Pragmatism: Rethinking the Relationship of Ethics and Epistemology* (Routledge, 2021).

Why It's OK: The Ethics and Aesthetics of How We Live

ABOUT THE SERIES:

Philosophers often build cogent arguments for unpopular positions. Recent examples include cases against marriage and pregnancy, for treating animals as our equals, and dismissing some popular art as aesthetically inferior. What philosophers have done less often is to offer compelling arguments for widespread and established human behavior, like getting married, having children, eating animals, and going to the movies. But if one role for philosophy is to help us reflect on our lives and build sound justifications for our beliefs and actions, it seems odd that philosophers would neglect arguments for the lifestyles most people—including many philosophers— actually lead. Unfortunately, philosophers' inattention to normalcy has meant that the ways of life that define our modern societies have gone largely without defense, even as whole literatures have emerged to condemn them.

Why It's OK: The Ethics and Aesthetics of How We Live seeks to remedy that. It's a series of books that provides accessible, sound, and often new and creative arguments for widespread ethical and aesthetic values. Made up of short volumes that assume no previous knowledge of philosophy from the reader, the series recognizes that philosophy is just as important for understanding what we already believe as it is for criticizing the status quo. The series isn't meant to make us complacent about what we value; rather, it helps and challenges us to think more deeply about the values that give our daily lives meaning.

Titles in Series:

Why It's OK to Be a Gamer

Why It's OK to Mind Your Own Business

Justin Tosi and Brandon Warmke

Why It's OK to Be Fat

Rekha Nath

Why It's OK to Be a Gamer

Sarah C. Malanowski and Nicholas R. Baima

Selected Forthcoming Titles:

Why It's OK to Be a Socialist

Christine Sypnowich

Why It's OK to Be a Moral Failure

Robert B. Talisse

For further information about this series, please visit: www.routledge.com/Why-Its-OK/book-series/WIOK

SARAH C. MALANOWSKI AND
NICHOLAS R. BAIMA

Why It's OK
to Be a Gamer

Routledge
Taylor & Francis Group

NEW YORK AND LONDON

Designed cover image: © Andy Goodman

First published 2024
by Routledge
605 Third Avenue, New York, NY 10158

and by Routledge
4 Park Square, Milton Park, Abingdon, Oxon, OX14 4RN

Routledge is an imprint of the Taylor & Francis Group, an informa business

© 2024 Sarah C. Malanowski and Nicholas R. Baima

The right of Sarah C. Malanowski and Nicholas R. Baima to be identified as authors of this work has been asserted in accordance with sections 77 and 78 of the Copyright, Designs and Patents Act 1988.

All rights reserved. No part of this book may be reprinted or reproduced or utilised in any form or by any electronic, mechanical, or other means, now known or hereafter invented, including photocopying and recording, or in any information storage or retrieval system, without permission in writing from the publishers.

Trademark notice: Product or corporate names may be trademarks or registered trademarks, and are used only for identification and explanation without intent to infringe.

Library of Congress Cataloging-in-Publication Data
Names: Malanowski, Sarah, author. | Baima, Nicholas R., author.
Title: Why it's ok to be a gamer / Sarah Malanowski and Nicholas R. Baima.
Other titles: Why it is ok to be a gamer
Description: New York, NY : Routledge, 2024. | Series: Why it's ok: the ethics and aesthetics of how we live | Includes bibliographical references and index.
Identifiers: LCCN 2023050140 (print) | LCCN 2023050141 (ebook) | ISBN 9781032312156 (hardback) | ISBN 9781032312132 (paperback) | ISBN 9781003308638 (ebook)
Subjects: LCSH: Video gamers—Psychology. | Video games—Social aspects. | Violence in video games.
Classification: LCC GV1469.34.P79 M36 2024 (print) | LCC GV1469.34.P79 (ebook) | DDC 794.801/9—dc23/eng/20231228
LC record available at https://lccn.loc.gov/2023050140
LC ebook record available at https://lccn.loc.gov/2023050141

ISBN: 978-1-032-31215-6 (hbk)
ISBN: 978-1-032-31213-2 (pbk)
ISBN: 978-1-003-30863-8 (ebk)

DOI: 10.4324/9781003308638

Typeset in Joanna and Din
by Apex CoVantage, LLC

Sarah dedicates this book to her mom, for her unwavering support and her permission to play Game Boy at the dinner table

Nicholas dedicates this book to the greatest gamer of all time—Chris

Contents

Acknowledgments

We thank Andrew Beck and Marc Stratton for seeing the value in this project and for their support throughout it. A number of people have provided helpful feedback on this project; we thank: Emily Austin; Eric Brown; Anna Christensen; Tobias Flattery; Jeremy Garcia-Diaz; Ashley Kennedy; Rachel Luria; Tyler Paytas; Jeremy Reid; Clerk Shaw; Christopher Strain; the Wake Forest Philosophy Department; participants of the Wilkes Honors College of Florida Atlantic University of Ethics of Video Games Conference; the students in Nich's Philosophy of Video Games class—in particular, Gwen Murray, Joey Rohe, and Kelland Earle Timothy—as well as all our students who read various drafts and provided feedback. We thank the Wilkes Honors College of Florida Atlantic University for generously funding a new gaming computer and sponsoring the Ethics of Video Games Conference. We thank Michael McNeill for his illustrations, and Neil Dowden for copyediting.

Finally, we thank our friends and family. Sarah thanks her guild ACORNS for the laughs, frustration, and memes—much of her contribution to this book is inspired and informed by them—and Nich for encouraging this project and patiently enduring Sarah's penchant for excessively exceeding the word limit.

Nich thanks his gamer friends: Rex, Rup, and Takedown; noble Delta and wise Athena, faithful companions; and Sarah, with love.

Introduction

> In matters of this sort, it isn't enough just to assume these things; one needs to investigate carefully by means of argument, for the investigation concerns the most important thing, namely, the good life and the bad one.
>
> Socrates, Plato's *Republic* 9.578c

According to recent surveys, three billion people worldwide play video games. In the United States, roughly two-thirds of adults and three-fourths of children play, with just over 50% identifying as male and just under 50% identifying as female. The video game industry now makes well over 100 billion USD in revenue, surpassing the global film industry.[1] Yet, despite the popularity of gaming, there is a stigma attached to it. The "gamer" stereotype is still very much a part of our culture: when we think of gamers, we often have in mind the greasy, unkempt adult male living in his parents' basement—lazy, socially awkward, inept, and unable and/or unwilling to progress through the important life stages that typically signify success. More disturbingly, video games are often associated with violence. Although studies have repeatedly failed to establish a clear causal connection between playing violent video games and committing acts of violence, the narrative that video games promote violent tendencies continues to be repeated in the media and by prominent and influential people. In addition to worries about video games causing violent

DOI: 10.4324/9781003308638-1

behavior, the gaming community has a reputation for being a social space filled with rage, racism, sexism, and general immaturity—not the type of behavior most people want to be associated with.

Additionally, there is increasing concern about the amount of time children and adults are spending on "screens." Video games certainly contribute to this growing amount of "screen time," and thus it is important to consider whether this is time well-spent. Furthermore, there is legitimate concern over the potential for video games to be addictive: the World Health Organization has added "gaming disorder" to its International Classification of Diseases, and the American Psychological Association now considers gaming addiction as a possible condition to include in future editions, pending further study. The Chinese government has recently banned gamers under the age of 18 from playing during the week and restricted playing on the weekends to between 8 PM and 9 PM out of concern regarding addiction, negative health implications, and Western ideological influence.[2]

Gamers are thus often associated with various vices like rage, immoderation, immaturity, and laziness. Society rarely extols the positive aspects of gaming, but the recent attention on video games has not been all negative. The COVID-19 pandemic has demonstrated first-hand to many people the important social role that video games can play: when much of the world's population was unable to socialize in person, video games offered a way for people to connect with one another and still do fun activities together. With this in mind, and with the increasing number of people who embrace the gamer identity, we think we are at a point in time in which it makes sense to explore the virtues of the gaming lifestyle. In this book, we explore the possibility of being a virtuous gamer *qua* gamer—that is, the ways in which being a gamer can help one cultivate and exemplify virtue. We argue that there are many ways in which games can help us flourish. We show how playing video games can help us develop both ourselves and our relationships with others, give us a unique aesthetic experience, provide us with psychological benefits, and just plain help us relax and enjoy ourselves. Video games are not just for those with no life; on the contrary, they can help contribute to a rich and meaningful life.

VIRTUE THEORY

This book examines the ethics of gaming from a virtue theoretic approach inspired by ancient Greek and Roman philosophy and informed by contemporary psychology. We don't swear allegiance to any one philosopher or school of thought, but rather we look for inspiration from a wide range of ancient Western virtue thinkers, such as Socrates, Plato, Aristotle, Cicero, Seneca, Epictetus, Marcus Aurelius, and even the pleasure-loving Epicurus. Although these philosophers disagreed with each other over technical differences, they largely agreed that (a) ethics fundamentally aims at *eudaimonia*, or the good life, and that (b) *aretē*, or virtue, is fundamental to living well. By briefly looking at these two concepts (*eudaimonia* and *aretē*), we will show why we prefer a virtue theoretic approach for the topic at hand.

The Greek concept of *eudaimonia* encompasses both subjective and objective aspects of a good life: the inwardly feelings of happiness and the outwardly markers of success. Thus, achieving *eudaimonia* means that one is living a happy and successful life. Unlike our contemporary concepts of "well-being" and "happiness," though, *eudaimonia* applies to a lifetime, not mere moments or periods of one's life. As Aristotle explains, just as one nice day doesn't mean that winter is over and spring has arrived, "a brief period of happiness doesn't mean one is supremely blessed and happy."[3] For the sake of simplicity, going forth we will refer to *eudaimonia* using the English words "happiness," "success," and "well-being"; however, it is important keep in mind its broader notion.

Now you might worry that an ethical theory which gives pride and place to one's own happiness is overly selfish (after all, isn't ethics about how we should treat others?). However, the concept of *aretē*, or virtue, mitigates worries about brute egoism. The ancient virtue theorists thought that there was a close connection between happiness and *aretē*, which refers to excellent human character traits, or virtues. To lead a fulfilling life, they believed that one must cultivate excellence in character and conduct, not only by treating others appropriately but also by feeling the appropriate sentiments toward them. A virtuous person, for instance, wouldn't begrudgingly treat someone fairly, but would take pleasure in doing this because they care about justice and fairness.

The Greek word *aretē* is usually translated as "virtue," and we will follow suit. Nonetheless, it is crucial to bear in mind that just as *eudaimonia* doesn't quite mean the same thing as our word "happiness," *aretē* doesn't quite mean the same thing as our word "virtue," as *aretē* can refer to excellence more generally, whereas our word "virtue" solely refers to "moral excellence." For instance, *aretē* can apply to clearly non-moral things like flute-playing, horse-riding, and eyeballs, but today we don't refer to people as being virtuous for their skills with musical instruments and no one uses the expression the "virtue of eyes," as Plato did.[4] Consider Sharon, who is both an excellent flute player and a kind and generous person. Today, we would only consider her virtuous because of her kindness and generosity—her aptitude for lip aperture would not factor into the equation. But for the ancients, Sharon's skill in flute-playing could meaningfully contribute to thinking she is a virtuous, or excellent, human being. So, whereas today virtue has a narrower moral connotation, in the past it referred to excellence more generally.

Now the ancient virtue theorists didn't think that flute-playing was the key to happiness (though they did have a surprisingly a lot to say about it—Aristotle, for instance, thought the flute was too exciting an instrument).[5] However, they did think that the "cardinal virtues" (courage, moderation, wisdom, and justice) were centrally important to flourishing. But they were also concerned about character traits that are largely outside the purview of moral philosophy today. Aristotle, for instance, thought there was a virtue of gracious playfulness which involves the right degree of wit (see Chapters 2 and 6). The virtues, then, aren't just the traits that make us morally good individuals, but rather those characteristics that make us excellent overall.

This last point demonstrates a fundamental distinction between moral discourse today and ancient ethics. In modern moral discourse, there is a line between the moral and nonmoral. It might be bad to be a humorless grump, but it is hardly immoral. The moral, according to contemporary thought, focuses on the concepts of right and wrong and permissible and impermissible, and it seems a bit too strong to say that it is wrong or impermissible to be humorless and grumpy. Though these traits are unpleasant, they are scarcely harmful. In contrast, because the ancient virtue ethicists were interested in how one should live generally, being humorless and grumpy can be assessed ethically. If we are thinking what virtues or character dispositions would make one an awesome human being, then it is reasonable to consider what role humor and grumpiness play. Grumpy might be your favorite of the "seven dwarfs," but he seems like a much more difficult individual to engage with than Doc, Happy, or Sneezy. What this demonstrates is that virtue theory is concerned with a much broader ethical assessment than modern moral thinking.[6]

It is this broader approach that we think makes virtue theory especially suited to addressing ethical questions concerning video games. Though there are some narrow moral concerns about video games and violence, many ethical issues surrounding video games involve whether it is a worthwhile activity. For instance, some people today think that adults playing video games are wasting their time. Since it is generally thought not to be wrong or impermissible to waste time, the modern moral approach would treat this as a non-moral issue—something outside the scope of morality, much like being a grump. However, because the virtue ethics approach examines what type of life is worth living and what traits such a life involves, whether something is a waste of time or worthwhile pursuit is centrally important. It might not be immoral to devote your life to baseball cards, but is it a life well-lived? Accordingly, when we ask if it's OK to be a gamer, we aren't asking if it is *permissible* to be a gamer—it surely is—but rather whether being a gamer contributes to or detracts from living well.[7]

That explains why we prefer the virtue theoretic approach, but why an *ancient Greek and Roman* virtue theoretic approach? Two reasons. First, one of us (NB) studies ancient Greek and Roman ethical theory; so, this is the version of virtue theory that we are most familiar with and the one we are most interested in talking about. Second, we are largely sympathetic to what these philosophers say and their general approach to philosophy. These thinkers believed that philosophy should having something to say about how we live, and we believe that there is often great wisdom to be found in their writing.[8]

OK, but why an ancient virtue theory approach informed by *contemporary psychology*? Two reasons motivate this as well. First, one of us (SM) is a philosopher of cognitive science. Second, some of the reasons for thinking that being a gamer isn't OK are tied to contemporary neuroscience and psychology, such as the claims that violent games promote aggression (Chapter 1) and can be addictive (Chapter 5). Addressing these concerns requires diving into some of the details of science. Though our contemporary psychological methods have developed since ancient times, ancient ethical theory was informed by their view of human psychology. Accordingly, applying psychology to virtue theory is well within this tradition.

There are many acceptable approaches to an ethical analysis of video games, and each approach has various advantages and disadvantages. We by no means intend to suggest our approach is the best full stop; rather, we believe our approach is the best for *us* given our background and the questions we are interested in exploring.

Before we close this section, it is important to address what might be a potential concern. The ancient virtue theorists saw that virtue was connected to happiness, but this connection is far from intuitive. Why think that living well requires being a good human being? A complete answer to this question (if that is even possible) would itself require a lengthy book. That said, we can offer a brief consideration for thinking that virtue is connected to happiness. We can all agree that being emotionally disturbed and making terrible choices negatively affects our happiness. It is hard to feel happy when you are frustrated, angry, ashamed of the choices you make, and live in a constant state of competition and conflict with others.

In contrast, being tranquil, proud of the decisions you make, and living in harmony with others feels good. The virtues lead us toward the latter, while the vices the former. For instance, justice allows us to relate to others in an appropriate way, wisdom guides us in making sound choices, moderation balances our desires in a rational way, and courage permits us to take pride in the decisions we make.

To further illustrate the connection between happiness and virtue and unhappiness and vice, consider Ebenezer Scrooge. Despite having an absurd amount of wealth, Scrooge was a curmudgeon. He had subordinates who feared him, but no (living) friends. His greed helped him accumulate affluence, but his financial freedom didn't make him free from desire; rather, his avarice trapped him into a life of hoarding and restless acquisition. However, when he came to see the errors of his way and began to love and care about others, he progressed toward happiness.

OF GAMES AND GAMERS

This is a book about gamers, but who is that? There are all sorts of games, after all, and countless internet fights have been had over who counts as a "real" gamer, so perhaps you want us to define what exactly we mean by "gamer." If so, you are in good company: in Plato's dialogues, Socrates, the ancient Greek philosopher (you may also know him as the philosopher in *Assassin's Creed Odyssey*), is often concerned with defining terms. For example, he aims to discover the nature of virtue by posing "What is X?" questions (for example: What is courage? What is moderation? What is piety?) to people who claim to know. The dialogues then typically proceed as follows: the person offers an answer, Socrates claims that the answer doesn't work because it was only an example of the virtue rather than a definition, the interlocutor tries again and Socrates refutes this answer, repeat a few times, and eventually the dialogue ends in *aporia*, or puzzlement, with no determinate answer reached.

The 20th-century philosopher Ludwig Wittgenstein commented that "[r]eading the Socratic dialogues one has the feeling: what a frightful waste of time! What's the point of these arguments that prove nothing and clarify nothing?"[9] Wittgenstein believed that a precise attempt to answer the "What is X?" question was a fool's errand, because it assumes that there is a determinate essence that connects all uses of X, but no such essence actually exists. For this reason, he held that his own view

> is the antithetical standpoint to the one occupied by Socrates in the Platonic dialogues. For if I were asked what knowledge is, I would enumerate instances of knowledge and add the words "and similar things." There is no shared constituent to be discovered in them since none exists.[10]

Though we wouldn't go as far as Wittgenstein and hold that the method of the philosophical star of *Assassin's Creed Odyssey* is a "waste of time," we do think Wittgenstein was correct that that examples are helpful and sometimes all you need. So, rather than try to give a definition of what we mean by video game and gamer, we believe that it will be more helpful to provide some examples of what we have in mind.[11]

When we talk about gamers, what we mean is people who consider it their hobby to play video games like *World of Warcraft*; *Mass Effect*; *Uncharted*; *Minecraft*; *Apex Legends*; *The Last of Us*; *Super Smash Brothers*; *Rocket League*; *Red Dead Redemption*; *BioShock*; *League of Legends*; *God of War*; *Gone Home*; *Cuphead*; *FIFA*; *Zelda: Breath of the Wild*; *Portal*; and *Life Is Strange*. The list is far from exhaustive, but it includes video games produced by large and small studies; role-playing games (RPGs); action and adventure games; platforming games; competitive shooters; massive multiplayer online games (MMOs); story-driven games; sports games; and sandbox games (i.e. games that are less about achieving a specific goal, but are more about exploration and creativity, sort of like you are playing in a sandbox).

Intentionally absent from the list are (a) educational games, word/puzzle games, and digitized physical games (e.g., Duolingo, Sudoku online, chess online) and (b) extremist games (e.g. white supremacist games, terrorist games, rape fantasy games). Our goal in this book is to explore the ethics of gaming from the typical gamer's perspective. The games in category (a) are not within that scope—if someone habitually plays online chess or Wordle, they typically do not refer to their hobby as video games. The games in category (b) are far from mainstream, and we have no interest in defending games that have clearly abhorrent content (we'll say more about that in Chapters 1 and 2).

ROAD MAP

Our strategy for showing that being a gamer can contribute positively to the good life is a kind of "intellectual aikido": each chapter will begin with what is thought to be a commonly held critique of gaming, then we will attempt to reverse this "attack" by showing how it is misguided or at least not the full story, and how it can give way to a positive aspect of gaming. Despite our defense of gaming, we don't think everything about gaming is rosy—there are aspects of gaming that are bad and segments of gamers that are prone to toxicity. Hence, our thesis is that, although there are legitimate concerns over video games, some of them are exaggerated or ill-founded, and they can mask the positive effects that gaming can have on us. Not only is gaming generally OK, but when it is done right, it contributes to a virtuous and flourishing life.

Chapter 1 begins by examining the perennial worry that violent video games contribute to violent tendencies. If violent video games promote violence, then those who aspire to be virtuous gamers would presumably need to remove these titles from their game library. This wouldn't be such a big deal if video game violence were a rare occurrence, but this isn't the case: the brutal killing of enemies is a pervasive focus of gameplay, and some of the most critically acclaimed games, such as the *BioShock* and *Mass Effect* series, include violence. After assessing the evidence, though, we argue that it isn't sufficient to support the claim that playing violent games causes violent behavior. However, we also argue that this doesn't give gamers the green light to play any game or to play any way they want—virtue requires that we play appropriately. The result is that, although violent video games need not be categorically excluded from Socrates' game library, those games must have some redeeming aesthetic/intellectual quality that justifies the use of violence.

One thing the violence objection gets right is that our in-game behavior *matters*. But narrowly focusing on the violent content of video games has stunted more general ethical discussion of gaming, as it distracts from more realistic potential vices and overlooks the potential for virtue. In Chapter 2, we develop a taxonomy of virtues and vices in gaming that expands the ethics of gaming to include consideration of how playing video games can develop or hinder excellent character traits. We argue that just as athletics can develop both virtue and vice, so can gaming. When done well, gaming can help develop the virtues of tolerance, appropriateness, chillness, fortitude, honesty, humility, kindness, and moderation, but when done poorly, gaming can contribute to the vices of gate-keeping, tryhardedness, rage, fragility, dishonesty, ego, toxicity, and immoderation.

Chapter 3 addresses the stereotype that gamers are loners. Since friendship is clearly part of the good life (as Epicurus puts it, "friendship dances around the world announcing to all of us that we must wake up to its blessedness"), if gaming hinders the development of friendship, then this would be a serious reason to put down the controller and pursue more social activities instead.[12] Although many games are social, multi-player experiences, some critics worry that these gaming relationships are artificial and displace potential genuine in-person friendships. Nevertheless, drawing upon Aristotle's account of friendship, we argue that gaming friendships can constitute genuine friendships. Indeed, we argue that gaming is an excellent way for adults to develop friendships with people from diverse backgrounds.

Undoubtedly, many gamers have had the experience where they tell themselves, "I'll just do one more quest," but one quest turns into two, and before you know it, several hours have passed. Such extended playing sessions often come at the cost of much needed sleep, exercise, homework, and time spent with loved ones. Games have an amazing ability to suck us in, so much so that many psychologists today worry that gaming is addictive. Chapter 4 examines these claims and argues that the addiction model isn't the best way to think about problematic gaming because problematic gaming differs from other objects of addiction in important ways. That said, there are features of modern games that resemble gambling, and we argue that the onus is on developers to remove these features from games. We end the chapter by arguing that far from "frying" your brain, gaming has many cognitive benefits.

Setting aside worries about violence, sociability, and addiction, many people worry that gaming is a waste of time. As Catholic Father Donald Calloway puts it:

> As a norm, adults should not be playing video games; their leisure moments should be more dignified and age appropriate. It's so sad today to see how many grown men live in a fantasy world of video games; waste of time and money. No woman I know delights in dating and/or marrying a man who sits on his duff all day pushing buttons frantically like a lunatic.[13]

Simply put, many think the adult gamer is a "manchild" who eschews their responsibilities to engage in a worthless childish pastime (despite the fact that there are many female gamers today, the maleness of the gamer identity still lingers like the remnants of a dissipating fart). In Chapter 5, we argue that this manchild objection involves a myopic view of both value and games. It is based on a narrow-minded view of value that ties the worth of an activity to its outcome, overlooking the intrinsic value of the activity itself. It also assumes a parochial view of games that ignores their aesthetic and intellectual qualities. From interactive fictions to simple platforming games, video games can encourage creativity, provoke imagination, and fill us with a sense of wonder. Just as we shouldn't think reading novels, studying philosophy, and wandering through an art museum is a waste of time, we shouldn't think gaming is either.

Throughout Chapters 1–5, we justify the gamer life by arguing that gaming provides a venue for developing virtue, making friends, and letting your imagination and creativity run wild. Though we believe that the justification we provide is

Why It's OK to Be a Gamer

Image 0.1 Map of the reader's journey

true and important, in Chapter 6 we argue that there is danger in *needing* to justify gaming on these further grounds. Play, of which playing video games is a part, is a fundamental human good. So, while it is true that video games can help us develop virtues and provoke intellectual and aesthetic experiences, playing games *requires* no further justification beyond the inherent value of play itself. Indeed, having the appropriate attitude toward play is an important character trait.

AUDIENCE, SOURCES, AND MORE!

This book is intended for non-philosophers interested in exploring the merits of being a gamer from a philosophical perspective. More specifically, we have written the book with two target audiences in mind: (a) non-gamers who know gamers and (b) gamers. Why? Well, despite the immense growth in popularity of video games, we believe that both gamers and non-gamers alike misunderstand the nature of gaming as a hobby. In our society, there are many hobbies we see as valuable, but gaming is not one of them: non-guitar players, non-hikers, and non-cooks appreciate these activities, but the same isn't true about gaming. Non-gamers might tolerate their gamer loved one's hobby, but it is seldom appreciated or encouraged and shame is still very much attached to being a gamer. Hence, one goal of this book is to offer a concise account of the potential value of being gamer that is rooted in a hallowed tradition of intellectual thought.

Gamers themselves no doubt enjoy games and value games, but they too misunderstand their hobby, specifically its ethical dimension. Gamers tend to bifurcate their gaming self from their non-gaming self, or who they are "in real life" (IRL), and will then justify their mean or selfish in-game behavior on the grounds that it occurred while gaming, so it's "not real." Such an attitude is problematic for two main reasons. First, it falsely denies character and agency to your in-game self, as if how *you* act virtually doesn't affect others or have an influence on yourself IRL. Second, it contradicts an idea that resonates with many gamers: that gaming has value that goes beyond being mere mental distraction. As gamers, we can't argue that games are a source of genuine friendship and aesthetic experience while at the same time we claim that our in-game self isn't real. Accordingly, this book aims to show how gamers might consider the broader ethical dimension of gaming; that is, how gaming contributes to the development of self and reflects our "real" character. Once this is recognized, the sharp division between IRL and in-game breaks down. However, because this distinction is common internet parlance, we will use the term IRL to signify one's out-of-game self.

Because this book is written for non-philosophers, we have kept technical jargon and nuances of scholarly debates to a minimum. Pointers for more information can be found in the endnotes. Speaking of which, we as readers hate endnotes—flipping back and forth is a pain, and if the information is that important, it shouldn't be sequestered in the back and printed in reduced font. Accordingly, we have tried to keep endnotes to a minimum. For those weirdos who love endnotes, sorry! The translations we have used of older sources are listed in the references; however, some minor adjustments have been made to improve readability and understandability. We've also included some illustrations done by Michael McNeill, which we hope convey ideas in a humorous way. One last thing, when one of us wishes to interject our own experience, we use the expression (SM) for Sarah Malanowski and (NB) for Nicholas Baima; when we end long narratives, we use the phrase (SM out) and (NB out)—kind of like a walkie talkie. Alright, enough setup: take a sip of Mountain Dew and dust off your Cheeto fingers, because your adventure begins!

Fatality!

1

On violence and gaming

Then, as we said at first, our children's games must from
the very beginning be more law-abiding, for if their games
become lawless, and the children follow suit, isn't it impossible
for them to grow up into good and law-abiding people?

Socrates, Plato's *Republic* 4.424e–425a

Like the Grinch who stole Christmas, these violent video games
threaten to rob this particular holiday season of a spirit of goodwill.
Instead of enriching a child's mind, these games teach a child to enjoy
inflicting torture.

Senator Joe Lieberman, 1993 Congressional hearing

NB: It's Christmas Day, mid-90s, in the Chicago suburbs, and
the moment of truth is upon us. There is one remaining present: a joint gift to my brother and me from Grandma Marie
in the shape of a Sega Genesis game. But what game will it be?
It could be *Mortal Kombat*, which we asked for but our parents
expressed reservations about due to its violent nature. Or it
could be something like *Global Gladiators*—a McDonald's recy-
cling game in which the characters Mick and Mack combat
pollution. My brother, being older and bigger, muscles in front
of me and tears the wrapping off. To our surprise and joy, it
is the spine-ripping, blood-mode-enabled *Mortal Kombat*. As we
smile in front of our extended family, holding the game up
like a trophy, Grandma Marie voices hesitation, conflict, and
perhaps some shame. She explains that she heard on the news

DOI: 10.4324/9781003308638-2

that the game was violent, maybe even dangerous for children to play, but she knew it would make us happy, so she chose to get it. Was Grandma Marie's decision a good one? Were her worries well-founded? NB out.

In today's world of increasingly life-like graphics, VR, and 4K televisions, the violent images in Sega's *Mortal Kombat* are quaint. When Sub-Zero rips the spine out of his opponent, it looks like he pulls the spine out from behind his opponent, rather than from within. The lack of realism is silly and whimsical to the modern gamer, but at the time, Sub-Zero's finishing "spinal-rip" move, along with other iconic images like Johnny Cage coolly putting on a pair of sunglasses while pixelated red blobs of blood rain on the floor, were taken to be a harbinger for the collapse of society's morals. That such gory displays of violence were taken so lightheartedly and incorporated into children's games was a cause for concern for "Grandma Maries" worldwide. In Germany, *Mortal Kombat* was taken off the market; in Japan, the blood was changed to a green color to make it less realistic; and in the USA, it became a central example in the 1993 Congressional hearing on video game violence. In a woefully misguided attempt to placate these worries, when Nintendo ported the game to their Super Nintendo (SNES) system, they made some changes: blood was colored grey, some fatalities were made less graphic (e.g., rather than Johnny Cage uppercutting some poor bloke's head off, he now spears them with his foot), and aggressive terms were blunted (e.g., "fatality" was changed to "finishing") and playgrounds everywhere were filled with rumors on how to circumvent these changes.[1]

Worries about video games and violence further rose to prominence following the mass shooting at Columbine High School in 1999. After it became publicized that the perpetrators were fans of the first-person shooter game Doom, gaming became a routinely cited contributing factor to high-profile acts of violence. Belief in this supposed link between playing violent video games and violent behavior resulted in attempted legislation to ban the sale of violent video games to minors. Despite such legislation being struck down by the Supreme Court, the narrative that video games are danger-ous because they create violent tendencies continues to be repeated. Following the two mass shootings that occurred in one weekend in August 2019, President Trump declared that "we must stop the glorification of violence in our society. This includes the gruesome and grisly video games that are now commonplace."[2]

As illustrated in the epigraph, concerns about the media's effects on culture go back to Plato.[3] The basic idea is that the images we see, the stories we hear, and the virtual acts we com-mit via a controller shape who we are. Thus, if we spend our time committing and reveling in virtual immorality, then we, in turn, develop a propensity toward violence. Now the goal of this book isn't merely to argue that it is OK to be a gamer, but that gaming can contribute to a virtuous and meaning-ful life (eudaimonia). Hence, the first boss we must overcome is the 800-pound Donkey Kong that blocks our passage: the claim that there is strong psychological evidence linking play-ing violent video games to real-world violence—the "violence objection." If violent games contribute to violent tendencies, then it would be hard to argue that playing them could be part of a virtuous life. And since many, if not the majority of, mainstream games have some amount of violence in them, this concern threatens to severely limit the types of games compatible with virtue. This would be unfortunate as some of the most fun, complex, and thought-provoking games, like

Mass Effect, BioShock, and *The Last of Us*, have some elements of violence in them.

The idea that playing violent video games causes us to be violent is intuitively plausible. However, like any idea of its kind, it requires the support of scientific evidence. Although it sounds like something that could be true, that doesn't necessarily mean it is. It is thus important to ask whether such a link between violence and video games actually exists, and if it does, what is the nature of this link—that is, how exactly does playing video games contribute to real-world violence? After all, completing a mission of *Grand Theft Auto V* doesn't cause players *en masse* to put down their controller and punch someone in the face or kick a puppy, so whatever the relationship between video games and violent behavior is, it will not be a straightforward one. As it so happens, all the media attention on violent video games led to a flood of scientific investigations into the nature of the relationship between violent video games and violent behavior.

THE LEGACY OF CLOWN PUNCHING

Standing at the center of the claim that playing violent video games causes violence is a life-sized inflatable clown doll. Its name is Bobo, and the purpose of its unfortunate existence is to get punched by children for the sake of science. Albert Bandura and his colleagues will use Bobo to study how we learn aggressive behaviors by placing him in a room with an experimenter and a child participant.[4] The experimenter either will ignore Bobo and play peacefully with other toys, or they will begin physically and verbally assaulting Bobo while the child watches. The child will then be left alone in the room with Bobo and other toys while researchers observe what happens. The crucial question: will the children who saw the aggressive experimenter act more aggressively toward Bobo than the children who observed the peaceful experimenter?

Much to the dismay of Bobo and future fans of violent media alike, it turns out that the children who watched aggressive actions were more likely to play aggressively afterward: when children saw Bobo being kicked, punched, hit with a mallet, and jeered at, they did similar actions when they got their chance to be alone with Bobo, while the children who did not witness the abuse of Bobo very rarely initiated their own aggressive acts toward him during the free play period. This study was thus seen as a clear demonstration of the role of social learning in aggressive behaviors: we tend to imitate the behaviors that we see modeled to us.

The idea that playing violent video games causes aggressive behavior is a natural extension of the findings from the Bobo study: when the children see Bobo being beaten up, they are witnessing aggressive behaviors they likely wouldn't have seen otherwise, and when we play violent video games, we see many aggressive actions being performed that we also likely wouldn't have witnessed in daily life. Furthermore, we may have never thought to perform these actions had we not seen them being modeled to us. Just as taking a mallet to an inflatable clown's face might not have been something one would be inclined to do until they see someone else doing it (it does sound fun now that you've heard about it, doesn't it?), people might not be as prone to reacting with anger, hostility, violence, and even carrying out mass shootings if they have not seen this behavior (and even simulated it) in violent video games.

The Bobo study occurred before violent video games became the worldwide phenomenon that they are, and psychology's understanding of aggression has developed much since Bandura proposed his social learning model based on the study. However, the central conclusion that observing aggressive behavior teaches us to be aggressive became a basis for some of the most influential work on the effects of violent media. Psychologist Craig Anderson is one of the most prominent researchers on the effects of video game violence, and uncoincidentally happens to be one of the most vocal critics of violent video games. He once testified before the US Senate that "high exposure to media violence is a major contributing cause of the high rate of violence in modern US society."[5] His highly influential account of the causes of aggressive behavior, the "general aggression model" (GAM), incorporates aspects of the social learning model of aggression. It states, essentially, that we learn what counts as "appropriate" behavior and reactions via our environment. If we are repeatedly exposed to aggression, we internalize such behaviors and reactions as being normal and appropriate, and then when we encounter future situations, we draw on this knowledge to inform us on how to respond and thus end up responding aggressively.[6]

If aggressive behavior is largely the result of repeated exposure to aggression, as the GAM holds, then the idea that playing violent video games causes this behavior makes sense. If we spend a lot of time in a world of aggression, even if this world is virtual, we will internalize that this is normal, and that reacting aggressively is appropriate. The GAM, and by historical extension the Bobo study, has been a primary lens through which violent video games have been viewed by psychology, and much like how everything looks slightly blue when one wears blue-tinted glasses, the world looks a certain way when one "puts on" Bobo-colored glasses. However, if we take off our Bobo-colored glasses, things might appear differently.

THAT'S A SPICY MEATBALL

In order to examine the psychological evidence on violent video games, we need to clarify what psychologists mean by aggression and violence. Aggression is understood as behavior that is intended to harm, while violence is aggression that results in actual harm.[7] Aggression and violence thus exist on a continuum, with violence representing the extreme end of aggressive actions. All violent actions are thus acts of aggression, but not all acts of aggression are acts of violence.

Violent acts are relatively rare and cannot be ethically studied in a psychology lab (no review board would approve a study in which participants cause serious harm to others!). So most of the scientific study of the effect of violent video games has focused on the question of whether they cause an increase in aggression, rather than an increase in violence. However, the incidents that repeatedly push concerns about violent video games back into the public eye are acts of violence, and so we should already be a bit wary when, in the wake of these *violent* tragedies, the psychological evidence linking video games to *aggression* is touted, since violence is only a small subset of aggression according to the definitions used in this research. We will return to this point later, but for now, we will grant that an increase in aggressive behaviors that do not qualify as violence might be concerning.

When we look at the scientific literature that supports the claim that violent video games increase aggression, the games look quite problematic. In fact, at the time of writing, the American Psychological Association's resolution on violent video games holds that:

> [S]cientific research has demonstrated an association between violent video game use and both increases in

aggressive behavior, aggressive affect, aggressive cog-
nitions and decreases in prosocial behavior, empathy,
and moral engagement . . . [and] all existing quantitative
reviews of the violent video game literature have found
a direct association between violent video game use and
aggressive outcome.[8]

Sounds pretty bad! However, before we burn all copies of
Call of Duty and Mortal Kombat in the hope of making the world
a more peaceful place, we should examine what this claim
really means.

The core challenge of researching violence and video games
is demonstrating whether there is a *causal* relationship between
playing video games and aggression. This is where experimental research becomes important: in order to demonstrate
that doing X causes Y, the most basic thing we need to do is
set up an experiment in which subjects do X, and then measure the change in Y, so that we can see if doing X is what
actually causes the change in Y. In this case, we would need to
have subjects play violent video games and then measure the
change in aggression afterward.[9]

However, demonstrating causal relationships in psychology
is quite tricky. It is particularly difficult when the behavior you
want to study is aggressive behavior. When you think about
the behaviors you would say exemplify aggression, you probably have in mind situations like someone starting a bar fight
after the bartender gets their drink wrong or someone dangerously cutting off a slower driver on the road. But these types
of aggressive behaviors are hard to measure in a psychology
lab, since they are evoked in complex real-world scenarios,
where scientists are not watching. Furthermore, even if such
scenarios could be replicated in the lab, it would be highly

unethical to subject experimenters and participants to situations designed to provoke dangerous, aggressive behaviors.

Because researchers cannot study paradigmatic aggressive behaviors in the lab directly, they measure various physiological proxies for aggression—the changes in the body that happen when one acts aggressively, such as elevated heart rate, sweaty palms, or increased cortisol levels—instead of aggressive behaviors themselves. The meaning of aggression here is thus changed from "aggressive behavior" to "measurable bodily changes that often occur when people are being aggressive." This type of study typically finds that playing violent video games increases all these physiological markers of aggression, and so researchers might claim that violent video games cause aggression, in the restricted way they have defined aggression.[10]

Of course, having sweaty palms does not mean one will act aggressively, and elevated heart rate is caused by doing exciting things in general. Thus, such studies do not provide very convincing evidence of the causal relationship between violent video games and actual aggressive behavior, so the redefining of "aggression" to mean those physiological proxies seems more than a bit disingenuous.

Recognizing this, other studies attempt to create situations where participants can actually exhibit aggressive behaviors or thoughts following video game play. But because it would be unethical to allow subjects to be overtly aggressive, experimenters design situations in which participants have the opportunity to do very tame acts of "aggression." For example, participants might play a video game, and then afterward be asked to blast a noise at another person. People generally do not like having loud noises blasted at them, and so if participants who play violent games blast louder noises than those who play non-violent games, then researchers might conclude that violent games cause more aggressive behaviors.[11] Here, "aggression" has been redefined to mean something more like "mildly annoying behaviors." The issue with this is that this type of "aggression" is not really something that we as a society need to be overly concerned about. Furthermore, these are short-term effects—there is little reason to assume that the temporary increase in "aggression" elicited by a single event will translate to more aggressive behaviors in the future.

The core issue with the use of multiple definitions of aggression in psychological research, then, is that the conclusions drawn from these studies lack teeth. After playing a violent video game, you might have elevated heart rate and higher blood pressure, be temporarily prone to blast louder noises, have more aggressive thoughts, and mix spicier hot sauces for spice-dislikers to taste (yes, this was a real study), but these actions are not obviously wrong, and none of them entail that you will commit actual acts of violence in the future. This data certainly does not seem like a sufficient basis for a society-wide moral alarm (unless, perhaps, you *really* hate loud noises and spicy food).

ICE CREAM SALES AND DROWNINGS ON THE RISE

Given the difficulties in translating the findings from experimental data to plausible claims about how exposure to violent video games affects real-world violence (that is, the lack of *external validity* in such studies), researchers also utilize a second strategy for establishing the link between violent video games and violent behavior: they look at existing trends between violent video game exposure and aggression and violent behavior. For example, in cross-sectional studies (i.e. studies that analyze data from a sample population at a given point in time), researchers ask participants how much or how often they play violent video games and then compare this to the amount of aggression (again defined in different ways depending on the study) the participant reports to have. If subjects who play violent video games have more aggressive behaviors and thoughts than those who do not play or do not play as often, then researchers might conclude that playing violent video games contributes to aggression. In longitudinal studies (i.e. studies that examine the same individuals for an extended period of time), researchers track a group of subjects over time, measuring both how much violent video game play and how much aggressive behavior occurs. If subjects who report more exposure to violent video games at the start of the study end up having more aggressive behaviors at the end of the study, then researchers might conclude that playing those games made the subject more aggressive over time.

Unsurprisingly, the data is mixed—some report associations between frequent violent video game play and aggressive behaviors, and some fail to find such associations at all.[12] However, *even* if the majority of studies did find evidence of such a relationship, this research would still only establish a *correlation* between violent video game play and aggressive behavior—it wouldn't establish that one *causes* the other. It's not enough to, as cross-sectional studies do, just look at a group of people who score high on measures of aggression and see how often they play violent video games, since it's possible (highly plausible, even) that aggressive people just happen to like those sort of games—their aggression issues might have existed prior to their video game use, and they might play violent video games simply because violence is more entertaining to aggressive people. The longitudinal data can get us closer to something that looks like a causal relationship, since it is tracking a change in aggressive behavior over time. However, it still cannot rule out factors other than violent video game play that might cause an increase in aggressive behavior over time.

The research on violent video game play and aggression thus finds itself stuck between a rock and a hard place. On the one hand, experiments that establish causal relationships can only tell us about "aggression" defined in various tame ways that are sometimes laughably divorced from real-world violence. On the other hand, the data that could perhaps tell us about the connection to actual aggressive behavior is not causal but correlative, and in the studies where such a correlation is found, the significance of that correlation is minuscule.[13]

BUT IS IT VIOLENT?

Notice that we have been assuming that there is a standard well-accepted account of what a violent video game is, but when you think about it a little, you will see that the concept is quite nebulous. There may be some paradigmatic examples of violent games (*Mortal Kombat, Grand Theft Auto*) and nonviolent games (*Animal Crossing, Just Dance, Tetris*), but most games fall somewhere in between—there is some violence throughout the game, but perhaps violence isn't the main focus of the game. If you ask someone what their favorite type of game is, it is unlikely they will respond, "Oh, you know, the violent ones." Games are not split up neatly into violent and non-violent; instead, game categories are typically based on gameplay style—the way the player interacts with the game (first-person shooter (FPS), racing, platformer, etc.). Although some game genres may tend to be more violent than others, many games from every category include some amount of violence.

And what counts as "violence" in the context of a video game, anyway? Is it the existence of realistic blood and gore, or do cartoonish interpretations, like teddy bears exploding into cupcakes on the Whimsyshire level of *Diablo III*, count? Is it just physical actions, or does casting spells and curses against others constitute violent action? Are racing games like *Mario Kart* violent—you can throw a turtle shell at other drivers or cause them to spin out by dropping a banana peel, after all—or are they just competitive? The cute aesthetic of the *Pokémon* games might lead one to categorize them as non-violent, but their gameplay centers on battling creatures against each other using very painful-sounding abilities like Guillotine, Flamethrower, and Acid Downpour until one becomes unconscious. Does it matter if the violence is done, as it is in many role-playing games, in the context of saving the world or protecting innocent civilians? Does it matter if it is a PvP setting vs a PvE setting?

Additionally, the amount of violence done in the game often depends on the way the individual player chooses to play. Many games offer a significant amount of player freedom in how to approach the game: sneak past enemies to get to the objective, or murder as many as possible along the way? Given the countless paths one can take in most games, it would be very difficult to quantify how much violence a particular game contains, since it depends on the individual playthrough.

These difficulties pose significant issues for the claim that playing violent video games causes aggression. For one, it makes consistency across studies difficult. If some researchers define the category of violent video games one way and others use a different definition, then there is little reason to think they are even researching the same thing. But if all the research uses only the paradigmatic examples of ultra-violent games, then there is little reason to think the findings will extend to the majority of games that include some violence but do not make it a focus.

Second, when we make a causal claim in science, like "smoking causes lung cancer," we want to specify what exactly is causing the outcome—in this example, the exact chemical compounds in tobacco smoke that are carcinogenic. But in the case of violent video games causing aggression, we can't pin down what specific aspects of violent video games are causing the aggression—"violent video games" is too broadly defined, and there are too many other aspects of gameplay that overlap with the broad category of games that include some aspect of violence. Games that have violence (however you define it) tend to be more exciting, more difficult and/or more competitive than games that do not contain any violence, and so it could simply be, for example, the increased difficulty of these games that leads to frustration-induced aggression. If researchers do not specifically control for these possibilities in their experiments (and many do not), then we simply cannot conclude that the violence itself in the game, never mind what kind of violence or how much, is what causes aggression.[14]

LET OUR POWERS COMBINE!

However, despite all these methodological difficulties and conflicting findings, the American Psychological Association still maintains that, when we look at all of these studies put together, video games are a cause for concern. Why do they say this?

The reasoning they employ here is based on what SM calls the *Captain Planet* approach to drawing scientific conclusions. For those of you who didn't grow up in the Golden Era of educational programming that was the 1990s, Captain Planet is a superhero who is summoned by five teens/pre-teens who combine the powers of individual elements together while saying the phrase "Let our powers combine!" Each element has different strengths and weaknesses, but when the children combine them, they are able to make a complete, powerful hero. A similar strategy is often employed in science: individual studies will often have different methodological strengths and weaknesses, but when we combine these studies together and they all point to similar conclusions, then the strength of one study can compensate for the weakness of another, and so on. For example, although the causal studies linking violent video games to aggressive behavior are weak in some ways and strong in others, the correlational studies are strong in ways that can cover the weaknesses of the causal studies and vice versa. Thus, if the majority of studies show some link between violent video games and aggression, then perhaps we can be confident that this link really does exist, even if there might be reason to question this conclusion in any one individual study.

Generally, putting together multiple lines of data to support a conclusion is a tried and trusted method in science. To use another "edutainment"-related analogy, just as you cannot build an elaborate Lego spaceship out of one Lego block, or even one type of Lego block, you cannot make a strong scientific claim with just one study, or just one type of study. If a scientist wants to find out if gases expand when heated, she cannot just form a conclusion based on heating one gas to one temperature in one type of container—she needs to heat up multiple different gases under many different conditions. Good science requires us to study whatever we are interested in under different conditions, with different types of measurements, in different populations, etc., before we can make a general claim that we can be confident about.

However, in the case of the violent video games and aggression studies, these studies shouldn't be combined to establish a generalization because each study is putting forth data on something slightly different from all the others, due to their differing definitions and questionable measures of aggression, failure to control for confounding variables, and little agreement on what counts as a violent video game. To return to the Lego analogy, it is like all the pieces being used aren't of the same kind—some are Lego, some are K'nex, some are digital Roblox, etc. They may share some superficial similarities, but it is hard to see how they could ever combine in the right way to build something bigger. Hence, the "powers combined" approach of the violent video game studies give us a heap of data without any clear generalization about their effects on real-world aggressive behavior to draw.

You might think we are, perhaps, being a bit too hard on the psychologists here. Many areas in psychology get stuck in the same hard place, and psychologists are aware of the limitations of their research. However, when it comes to an issue that garners a lot of public attention, has the potential to incite moral panic, affects public policy and courtroom decisions, is subject to political pressure, and concerns hundreds of millions of people, the epistemic demands for conclusions drawn should be great—a philosopher's way of saying, the data better be *really good*. But, when we look at that data, we see that not only are the conclusions mixed, but there are underlying methodological flaws in the research. Thus, the link between violent video games and violence is far from clear.[15]

ON GRANDMA MARIE'S WORRIES

So, what can we say about the claims on the news that worried Grandma Marie all those years back? The strongest and most concerning claim was that video games *cause* violence, but no obvious causal link between playing violent video games and violence has been established. The research is largely ambiguous, and at best it only shows a weak correlation between playing violent video games and violence. However, given that there are various alternative and plausible ways to explain this correlation, and given the methodological shortcomings discussed above, not much of anything can be drawn from this research.

Indeed, if playing violent video games actually did contribute to violent behavior, then we would expect violent crimes to increase as a population plays more violent video games. Given how popular and readily accessible violent video games and violent media, in general, have become, we should thus expect to be living in the most violent times of all. But, in fact, the opposite trend tends to be true. The countries that have the highest video game sales have lower levels of violent crime than countries where people play fewer video games (this finding holds even when other likely potential explanations for lower crime, like better economy and fewer adolescent males, are taken into account).[16] Furthermore, the rate of violent crime in the US has decreased as video games have increased in popularity, homicides tend to *decrease* in the months following the release of popular violent games, and the months with higher video game sales tend to have *lower* aggravated assaults.[17] Thus, if there is any relationship between widespread video game play and violent crime, then that relationship tends in the opposite direction of what the moral alarm over video games has suggested. Perhaps the solution to violent crime is *more* video games, not less. Of course, no one has ever claimed that violent video games are the sole cause of violent behavior (just as smoking cigarettes is not the sole cause of lung cancer), but if it really were the case that exposure to violent video games were a risk factor for future aggressive and violent behavior, then we should be able to discern some pattern linking increased video game use with increased violence (just as we can see a pattern linking increased smoking to increased lung cancer), but evidence of such a pattern simply does not exist.

If the stronger worry is that video games cause violence, then the weaker worry is that they are a risk factor for aggressive behavior. As we explained, the methodological problem with these studies is that there is a disconnect between the types of behavior the studies label as aggressive and the types of behaviors that motivated the studies in the first place. Grandma Marie wasn't worried about her great-grandchildren making loud noises and mixing spicier sauces—she already knew they were noise and hot sauce aficionados—she was instead concerned that they would get in trouble at school or become criminals. Put simply, it is unclear whether these behaviors or reactions really count as aggressive, and even if we grant that they do, it is uncertain that they lead to the types of aggressive behavior that are truly concerning.

In addition, it is important to bear in mind that there must always be a relevant comparison—are violent video games a risk compared to what? If violent video games are deemed too risky and their use is limited, some other activity must fill the void of time left behind, and there is no guarantee that these activities will be comparably better. Most of the things we do carry some risk, and it is unrealistic to expect people to spend their time only doing risk-free activities (if there even are any!). And even if there are less risky activities, they might have fewer potential benefits. Excluding games with any trace of violence or dark themes would limit the complexity of the stories we can tell through games, making them less engaging, artistic, and fun. So even if playing violent video games puts us at risk for aggressive behavior, we would still need to evaluate this risk and its potential benefits in comparison with the risks and potential benefits that alternative activities carry.

Finally, there are general methodological problems with the research. Psychologists are unable to distinguish all the individual nuances of gamers and the games they play (and it is hard to see how they will ever be able to do this). Of course, some video games focus entirely on committing violent acts, but games rarely include violence completely out of narrative context, and the games that do tend to be unpopular. Indeed, in many games, the violent acts a player might commit via an avatar are often put in a moral framework that the player is able to independently evaluate, and, as we will argue in Chapter 5, this affords gamers the opportunity for ethical contemplation.[18] Given that the category of "violent video game" is not uniform, and that the ways in which any particular gamer might play such a game are multitudinous, we find any general statement about the negative effects of playing violent video games to be, at best, incomplete and superficial, and, at worst, manipulative and deceptive.[19]

So, does that mean Grandma Marie's worries were unjustified? Unfortunately for gamers, it does not, at least not entirely. What it shows is that there is no clear evidence that video games cause violence or aggression. What it does not show is that video games have no negative influence on us, or that video games contain no negative values. Gaming could still be bad for us, even if it doesn't cause us to be violent. Hence, merely pointing out the dearth of empirical evidence linking video games to violence isn't enough to establish that it is OK—and it especially doesn't show that it is excellent—to be a gamer. Nonetheless, showing the limits of this research is an important first step to showing how gaming can contribute to the good life.

BEYOND NEGATIVE CONSEQUENCES

One thing the violence objection to gaming gets right is that gaming can impact who we are and how we act, and it can reflect both our best and worst traits. In general, the things that happen to us and the choices we make change us: activities you choose to pursue, circumstances put on you beyond your control, people you engage with both out of choice and out of necessity, etc., all shape who you are as a person. The virtual world may feel less "real," but things that happen to you in the virtual world still are ultimately processed by you and can, in turn, affect you. On the flip side, the virtual world is also a way of displaying who you are at your core. That is, not only are you affected by things while playing, but you yourself are an active participant in the game you are playing, and thus the actions you choose and the way you conduct yourself reflect who you are. Hence, even if there isn't psychological evidence that connects gaming to aggression and violence, what we do in a game ethically matters.

Perhaps you aren't convinced. Maybe you think it is just a game, so whatever you do while gaming doesn't matter (sometimes NB reaches out to players who "T-bag" and taunt him in game to inquire as to why they are displaying such hostility, and he is frequently met with "its juz a game bro don't cry"). In response, we'd ask you to consider a hypothetical game that centers on the horrible trio of torture, pedophilia, and racism. Imagine that it was firmly established beyond a doubt that playing games like this had no observable negative consequences. Despite the lack of obvious bad effects, many, if not most, would find something bad, or at least disturbing, about this game and those who choose to play it.[20] We wager that if someone listed playing these types of games as their hobby in their Tinder profile, you would swipe left, or if you found out that your significant other was a huge fan of this genre, an awkward conversation would ensue.

But notice, if your discomfort in these games is justified, it can't be on the grounds that they cause physical harm (since in our hypothetical situation, they do not)—it must be for some other reason. We believe that the uneasiness is best explained on virtue theoretic grounds. When we think about how we should feel, think, and act in a particular situation, we should reflect on what a virtuous agent would do and try to imitate them in a fitting way. For the moment, assume that gaming can be part of a virtuous life, and then ask yourself what types of games the virtuous agent would and wouldn't play. Though we may disagree about various details, we are confident we would all converge on the thought that the virtuous gamer doesn't play games that celebrate heinous acts and attitudes. This is because the activities we enjoy reflect our values, and valuing racism, rape, and pedophilia, even if it is just virtual in nature, is obviously not OK. Hence, taking pleasure in simulating these vicious acts and attitudes reveals bad aspects of our character.

In addition, the thought experiment assumes that gaming has no effect on us, but that is unrealistic. Video games are objects of culture and objects of culture represent and influence society. More straightforwardly, we spend money on video games; we get paid to develop them; we turn video game stories into movies, comics, and books; and we cosplay as video game characters. More abstractly, games, much like other forms of culture, shape and reflect what we think is beautiful, cool, and good. Indeed, the humanities are often defended on the grounds that they provide a humanizing function: not only can we learn about human nature through the humanities, but we actually develop more refined ethical thoughts and feelings through them. It is for this reason that the ancient virtue ethicists went to great pains in discussing the role of music, dance, stories, sports, and games in their culture. For the virtue ethicist, it isn't enough that we do the right thing, but that we also do it for the correct *reason* and feel the appropriate *emotion*, and culture can influence our reason and emotion.

Odysseus' navigation between two terrifying sea monsters in Homer's *Odyssey* provides a helpful image of the position we are staking out. On one side resides Scylla: an appalling monster with 12 tentacle-like legs, six long necks, each with its own head containing three rows of deadly teeth. Terrifying! But on the other side is Charybdis: a massive whirlpool creature who threatens to swallow entire ships. Like Odysseus and his sailors, gamers, too, must navigate between two dangers. On one side lurks the Charybdis of not considering the broader context of games, such as their fictional and playful nature, when assessing the gamer experience and its potential effects and value. However, in veering away from Charybdis, which gamers typically do out of love for their games, they risk falling victim to the Scylla of thinking that "it's only a game," and thus anything goes. This book attempts to sail between these two dangers. Killing a virtual being in game isn't an actual act of violence and we should be suspicious of someone who treats it as such. Having a funeral for the loss of a virtual character is an inappropriate response to their death. Nonetheless, this doesn't mean that in-game activities are devoid of ethical consideration altogether—our in-game life can still reflect and shape who we are.

Does this mean that violent video games and games with dark subject matters are off-limits to the gamer who aspires to be virtuous? Not necessarily. When thinking about violence and darker content from a virtue ethics perspective, the devil is in the details. How violence and dark material is presented matters. Is the violence portrayed in a realistic way or cartoonish way? Does the violence play an important aesthetic function? Is the violence situated in a moral framework? As we will discuss in Chapter 5, violence plays a key role in some of the most thought-provoking games, and the sterilization of these games would diminish their aesthetic and intellectual quality. After all, "moral transgression," Grant Tavinor notes, "might be a precondition of videogames becoming serious—and hence potentially challenging—art."[21]

Nonetheless, from the virtue theoretic perspective, it isn't just a matter of what you are playing, but how you are playing it and who you are. That is to say, when we think about the ethics of gaming, we also need to consider the motivational state, intelligence, and maturity level of the gamer. While the player fires a grenade launcher are they wishing this were real, or do they enjoy mastering in-game skills and find the story intriguing? Is the gamer too immature to understand the underlying moral themes, or does the gamer understand the fictional nature of the game and use the game as a tool for reflection or aesthetic appreciation?[22]

To help make sense of how we think of violence in video games, consider boxing. If the boxer enjoys inflicting pain on others and considers their craft an opportunity to legally hurt as many people as possible, then they have a vicious relationship to boxing. But if they see it as an opportunity to display a craft they love, to test their strength of spirit, to have a sense of brother/sisterhood, and to cultivate discipline, then it is a display of excellence. If this can be said about a craft in which people actually hurt one another, why couldn't the same be said of video games in which people only hurt virtual beings?

Violence in video games shouldn't be ignored, but focusing narrowly on the immorality of video game content blinds us from seeing the perhaps more realistic ways that gaming poses a threat to *eudaimonia*, as well as the ways it can help us make progress toward it. In the next chapter, we argue that gaming, like athletics, can help develop virtues by providing a venue for virtuous activity, but can also develop vice when done poorly.

KEY POINTS

- The violence objection holds that psychological evidence demonstrates that violent video games cause violence. If this objection is sound, then it severely restricts the types of games that could be compatible with a virtuous life.
- Aggression refers to the motivational behavior that aims at harm, while violence involves aggression plus actual harm.
- Since the types of aggression that clearly connect to violence cannot be studied directly in the lab, proxies are used instead. However, there are reasons to doubt that these proxies correspond in a meaningful way to the types of aggression that are worrisome.
- In examining the connection between violent video games and violence, researchers look at correlations between people who play violent games and people who commit violent acts. The evidence is inconclusive and limited in nature because correlation isn't causation.

- The Captain Planet "Let our powers combine!" approach to science involves combining different studies to generate a larger, more conclusive claim. However, a methodological hurdle is that different studies use different concepts of aggression and some are used in problematic ways. Thus, rather than producing the all-powerful combined general claim about violent video games, we get an amorphous heap of data.
- Overcoming the violence objection is the first step to showing that gaming can be part of the good life. However, overcoming this objection doesn't demonstrate that gaming is OK. The ethics of gaming goes beyond the empirically observable effects and includes our motivations and thoughts.

It is correct, then, to say that a person comes to be just from doing just actions and temperate from doing temperate actions; for no one has even a prospect of becoming good from failing to do them.

Aristotle, *NE* 2.4.1105b10–12

CHARACTER DEVELOPMENT IN SPORTS AND GAMING

"Although winning is part of sports, the ultimate purpose of sports is character development." Something like this is frequently stated across gymnasium floors—and it ought to be, for it is true. Most athletes who play sports will not reach an elite level in which they compete internationally or professionally. In addition, athletics is just one small aspect of life. They could be incredible athletes, but if they are heinous and miserable, it doesn't make sense to consider their life happy and successful, or *eudaimōn*. Indeed, there are countless examples of excellent athletes whose in-game success has failed to translate off the field, their life marred by bad decisions and a generally unlikeable persona. Accordingly, from the virtue ethics perspective, it is overly narrow to think of athletics as solely about triumph in sports. Rather, it makes much more sense to think of sports as having the higher aim of making us better through strengthening the body and mind.[1]

Though it is fairly obvious athletics develops the body, it might be less clear how it develops the mind. Sports provide

DOI: 10.4324/9781003308638-3

a relatively safe environment where we face situations that test our character. We are physically pushed, sometimes to our very limits. There are various psychological burdens as well: the fear of failure, the pressure that comes from family, friends, and teammates to excel, and the ever-encroaching desire to "win at all costs." And then there are the complex social dimensions to navigate: interacting with coaches, teammates, officials, fans, parents, partners, and fellow competitors. Hence, through sports, we can learn to overcome pain and adversity, face down fears, win and lose with grace, maintain integrity, be appreciative of others, and countless other things. These traits contribute to the development of virtue. For example, by learning to overcome adversity and fear, one progresses toward courage and fortitude. By learning to win and lose with grace, one advances toward humility. By learning to appreciate others, one moves toward gratitude and kindness. So, in sports, we learn life lessons and cultivate habits that help shape our character: when done well, we advance toward virtue; when done poorly, we regress toward vice.

The development of character isn't unique to athletics but applies to other "recreational" activities like art, dance, theater, music, and chess.[2] If this is not only true of athletics but extends to endeavors like chess and music, why wouldn't it also apply to recreational gaming?[3] Notice that the key difference can't be that gaming is less physically demanding, as not all typical character-cultivating recreational activities are physically challenging—gaming is as physical as chess and art, after all. Nor can the difference be that games don't require skill, but these other activities do, as games require strategy, intellectual flexibility, speed, and creativity. Indeed, mastering certain games requires a substantial investment in effort and time, and players treat gaming as if it were an activity attached to their identity. Just as one says, "I'm a pianist," another affirms, "I'm a gamer."

One might argue that the key difference is that video games are about having fun, but these other activities have other aims. However, each of these activities has many objectives, and we hope that, at least at the recreational level, fun is one of the aims of each of them. There is something sad about an athlete or musician who doesn't enjoy what they do. Furthermore, why would the fact that an activity aims at fun preclude it from cultivating character? One of the main motivations for virtue theory is that it broadens the scope of ethical consideration—rather than thinking of the ethics of an activity only in terms of harms and rights, we can think about how it contributes toward *eudaimonia*. In the virtue tradition, ordinary experiences—experiences that don't seem particularly moral—matter greatly.

You've probably heard the phrase, "It's not whether you win or lose; it's how you play the game." Although a cliché, it succinctly captures the association between game-playing and virtue. This association didn't just begin with motivational gym posters, though: the ancient Stoic Epictetus actually refers to Socrates as a "ball player." No, Socrates wasn't a "baller": by this, Epictetus meant that Socrates navigated life like an expert athlete—not forcing situations but moving with good judgment, agility, and strength, as well as with the cooperation of others.[4] What we need, according to Epictetus, is "the star athlete's concentration, together with his coolness, as if it were just another ball we were playing with too."[5] Epictetus' point is that we must treat life as a game. We needn't be so caught up with what we are playing and what the outcome is—that is largely outside our control—but we must focus on *how we play it*.

This lesson applies to everything in life. In another passage, for instance, he says:

> Whenever planning an action, mentally rehearse what the plan entails. If you are heading out to bathe, picture to yourself the typical scene at the bathhouse—people splashing, pushing, yelling and pinching your clothes. You will complete the act with more composure if you say at the outset, "I want a bath, but at the same time I want to keep my will aligned with nature." Do it with every act.[6]

Here, sage Epictetus advises us on how to handle the splish-splash of the surprisingly tumultuous public baths. A philosophical attitude is not just to be adopted in arguments and high-stakes moral decisions, but instead toward every action we do—gaming and baths included.

Not only does gaming matter because it is an activity in which we can develop and express our character, but relaxation and amusement are of central importance to living well, and it is for this reason that Aristotle maintained that there was a virtue pertaining to play. On the one hand, a person who lacks the ability to be playful is a bore and can ruin social engagements. But, on the other hand, the person who is obnoxiously playful is a buffoon. We, thus, ought to strive for a kind of gracious playfulness. (We will return to the importance of play in Chapter 6.)[7]

Putting these ideas together, we see that we ought to live as if life is a game, and we ought to game as if it is life. In other words, we ought to live with the grace, skill, intelligence, and levity of an expert ball player, and we ought to see our gaming self as being integrated into our larger character. Therefore, gaming provides a model for how to live, and our gaming self is an aspect of who we are and of central importance to life.

Gaming actually offers some unique character-building opportunities. It is quite easy to lose our minds and manners to rage and frustration while playing, and most multi-player gamers can attest that vicious behavior occurs with shocking frequency. Gaming psychologist Jamie Madigan attributes this to a number of key factors: anonymity; reduced self-monitoring and social accountability; and the transient nature of the social interactions.[8] This kind of situation resembles Plato's infamous "Ring of Gyges" thought experiment.[9]

In Plato's *Republic*, Socrates aims to show that it is always better to be just than unjust. Playing devil's advocate, Glaucon recounts the story of Gyges' ring. The story goes that a shepherd named Gyges discovered a ring that makes its wearer invisible—similar to gaming, when you wear the ring, no one can connect your actions back to your "real" self. Gyges used this power of invisibility to seduce the king's wife, kill the king, and take over the kingdom. Glaucon argues that anyone who came into possession of such a ring would perform unjust acts and that anyone who would refrain from injustice in such circumstances "would be thought wretched and stupid by everyone aware of the situation."[10] Glaucon takes this story to challenge Socrates' claim that it is always better to be just than unjust. If we have the power to benefit from injustice while escaping detection, then it would be foolish to not act unjustly. Hence, the true reason why we choose to act justly rather than unjustly is simply that we lack power—justice isn't our first choice but is only chosen when we can't get away with profitable wrongdoing. Thus, Socrates is tasked with showing that the person who acts unjustly with the ring is making a mistake with respect to their own self-interest. If he can do this, then Socrates will have shown strong evidence that it is always in our interest to be just.

Not only does the Ring of Gyges challenge Socrates to prove the inherent value of justice, but it also challenges the reader to reflect on *why* they care about morality. Do you act morally because you are worried about punishment and want the rewards of having a good reputation, or do you act morally because you intrinsically value justice? If it is the former, then you don't really care about justice *itself*—you merely want the positive things that come from *appearing* just and desire to avoid the negative things that come from appearing unjust. Gaming thus resembles the Ring of Gyges scenario, since we are anonymous and lack social accountability. As such, gaming provides both a way to test how we value virtue and a way to appreciate goodness itself.

In what follows, we explain how gaming can contribute to virtue by exploring eight main gaming vices (gatekeeping, tryhardedness, rage, fragility, dishonesty, ego, toxicity, and immoderation) and eight corresponding gaming virtues (tolerance, appropriateness, chillness, fortitude, honesty, humility, kindness, and moderation). This is not meant to be a definitive list—our aim is to highlight the aspects of virtue and vice that are most common in gaming. If you've played an online multiplayer game for a reasonable amount of time, we're confident you've encountered someone displaying these vices—alas, we ourselves have been guilty from time to time. That said, we are equally confident that you have also experienced displays of these virtues, though perhaps not as often—as Aristotle aptly notes, "There are many ways to error. . .But there is only one way to be correct. That is why error is easy and correctness is difficult, since it is easy to miss the target and difficult to hit it."[11] Because there are many ways to go wrong and vice is more common, we will spend more time discussing the vices. The hope is that by recognizing and understanding vice,

Table 2.1 Table of gaming vices and virtues

Dimension	Vice	Virtue
Acceptance of other players	Gatekeeping	Tolerance
Perspective of gaming	Tryhardedness	Appropriateness
Emotional temperament	Rage	Chillness
Dealing with adversity	Fragility	Fortitude
Truthfulness	Dishonesty	Honesty
Understanding of self and others	Ego	Humility
Social conduct	Toxicity	Kindness
Gaming consumption	Immoderation	Moderation

one can better understand the virtues. Though these virtues and vices are most clearly seen in online multiplayer games because of their social nature, much of what we say can apply to solo games. Additionally, our discussion of the intellectual and aesthetic value of gaming in Chapter 5 will more directly apply to solo play.

GATEKEEPING AND TOLERANCE

Gatekeeping in gaming can take several forms, but they all center on a player thinking that a game (or games in general) should be for a particular type of person (a type, presumably, shared with the gamer in question), and should be developed to cater to the needs and interests of people with those characteristics alone.

Perhaps the most common form of gatekeeping in gaming involves experienced players being condescending towards and unaccepting of new players—aka "noobs." In such cases, gamers are gatekeepers regarding skill, demanding that the game be designed with only "elite" players in mind and played only in a way that requires advanced skill, and may show general hostility to new or casual players, having no patience or tolerance for their lack of skill. In PvP, this often takes the form of saying that certain abilities or weapons, though perfectly legal and intentionally made by game designers, are "cheap" and that players are "trash" for using them. In PvE, this manifests in "elite" players not wanting lower-tiered players to get enjoyable in-game rewards. To be clear, there is nothing necessarily wrong with thinking that the excellence of the loot should be in proportion to the difficulty of the activity, but the way these critiques are frequently voiced is uncharitable and frankly hostile to new players.

Gatekeeping also occurs when players are upset that a game tries to appeal to a more diverse audience. The inclusion of characters with a variety of traits and backgrounds (e.g. minority races, genders, LGBTQ) can not only allow for different types of storylines, character development, and in-game relationships, but can also make the game more relatable to people who share those traits. For instance, some female players might not enjoy playing RPGs (role-playing games) that only give the option of being a male protagonist, because they might feel the behaviors, interests, and dialogue of the male protagonist are too dissimilar to their own. Nevertheless, if given the option of playing a female protagonist, the game can then be experienced in a more relatable way. (SM has, in fact, had this experience in playing the *Mass Effect* series and *Persona 3 Portable*, games in which choosing the female protagonist affects various aspects of the game.) Gamers who do not want a game to include these features so as to exclude others from the game are exhibiting the vice of gatekeeping. Of course, one can reasonably reject the expansion of playable characters for legitimate aesthetic reasons: perhaps developers are ham-fistedly changing core identities of the characters in order to have mass appeal or to make an ideological point—the details matter.

So, what's wrong with gatekeeping? There is nothing wrong in itself with being elite at a game, wanting to play with other elite players, or desiring that the characters, story, and gameplay go in a particular direction. Problems arise with the thought that the game should be meant only for you and cater only to how you (and those very much like you) envision the game. This is a selfish and narrow-minded view of a game. One of the greatest things about video games is that they appeal to a wide range of people because they are flexible enough to be enjoyed in various ways. Gatekeeping stifles this strength.

Additionally, the gatekeeper's behavior is often self-under mining. Gamers are passionate about their games and want them to thrive. But for games to thrive, they need to sustain a certain level of player population, which is largely maintained by the influx of new players, as well as casual gamers. So, the gatekeeper's negative attitude toward expanding the player base is often in tension with their love of the game. Noobs are needed, so you better be nice to them if you love your game.

Contrary to the vice of gatekeeping is the virtue of tolerance. In gaming, tolerance involves recognizing that everyone has a place in the gaming community—noobs and streamers alike—and that there are many different ways to enjoy the game. In order to be tolerant, we must recognize that the gaming community is larger than any one individual, and we must, as the Stoic emperor Marcus Aurelius recommends "practice really hearing what people say" and do our "best to get inside their minds."[12] Tolerance, however, doesn't require that we unreflectively accept the views of others, but it does require that we are receptive and open-minded.

TRYHARDEDNESS AND APPROPRIATENESS

The tryhard is sibling to the elitist. "Tryhard" is a pejorative term that refers to gamers who try harder than the nature of the activity merits. For example, if a game mode is designed for fun and casual play and a gamer treats it like the Olympics, they are being a tryhard. There is nothing wrong with putting effort into a game, though: there is fun to be had in improving one's gaming skills and mastering new techniques, and many game modes can't be undertaken without a concerted effort. In fact, striving to improve is itself a display of excellence. It would be a mistake to accuse someone of being a tryhard simply because they are trying, and many times when gamers accuse someone of being a tryhard, it is merely a reflection of their own insecurity and desire to be better at the game. Nevertheless, the person who takes the game too seriously and wants to win at all costs has lost sight of the fact that it is just a game.

This doesn't just apply to video games, either. One tradition of the Florida Atlantic University Honors College (where we teach) is the annual faculty vs. student softball game. The game is supposed to be about having fun and bonding. Unfortunately, sometimes the faculty forget this: we've seen and heard faculty members yell at each other for dropping balls and bench less experienced players. Contrast this with the students' approach, who welcome anyone who wants to play. Though winning is part of the game, it isn't the fundamental point of playing—the game is about bringing students and faculty together, and the attitude that some of the faculty adopted toward the game is antithetical to this purpose. Similarly, recreational gaming should be recreational, and anyone whose level of seriousness extends beyond this is not playing appropriately.

Tryhardedness can ruin entire game modes. Some game modes are designed for beginners and casual play. Knowing this, some tryhards go into the casual mode and "pubstomp" noobs and players aiming for relaxed play. The tryhards create a kind of arms race in which players who wanted to relax are now pressured to ramp up their intensity, and the poor noobs are obliterated. Tryhards can also ruin the gaming experience for their gaming group. Not every gaming team can play at a professional skill level, nor does every player want to approach the game with the level of seriousness required to play at that level, but that does not mean that they should not be playing the game. Tryhards fail to read the group's overall attitude toward the content when they demand that other group members focus on doing whatever it takes to maximize some aspect of gameplay (like damage output).

But is it wrong for the tryhard to game how they want? After all, they aren't breaking any formal rules. They are, however, breaking social norms in the game and, in doing so, making the game worse for everyone. In the case of the Pubstomping Tryhard, they're exploiting the social norms of play for their own benefit. In this way, the problem with tryhards is similar to the problem with line-cutters: when Joe cuts in line, he can only benefit if others agree to follow the norms of lines. If everyone decided to cut in line, it would be a "ring around the rosie" dance with no one advancing. Similarly, for a game to have casual modes of play, it must be the case that players treat the mode as casual and adjust their play accordingly. When tryhards violate this norm to get an edge on other players, they are taking advantage of the social agreement to play casually in that mode. If everyone were a tryhard, casual mode couldn't exist.[13]

If tryhardedness is the vice of *not having* the appropriate attitude toward a game, then the virtue is when one *has* the proper attitude toward the game. Unfortunately, there isn't a good name for this general state. The closest thing to it is "appropriateness" or "decorum."[14] Appropriateness, according to Cicero, includes being concerned about our "appearance and standing as a gentleman," as well as keeping "in mind the importance of the thing we wish to achieve, so that we employ neither more nor less care and effort than the case requires."[15] The latter means that the attitude that we should take toward an activity depends on the nature of the activity. And though much of the former aspect of appropriateness is antiquated (as much as we enjoy the idea of everyone putting on their gentlemanly attire before sitting down to game), there is still an element of truth worth retaining. When we think about how we should conduct ourselves, we should consider and respect others, and part of this involves thinking about how others behave and what they expect of us. If everyone walks on the right side of the sidewalk, we should have a good reason to walk on the left before we do so.

Appropriateness in gaming thus involves considering and respecting how others are playing. Like the sidewalk example, this doesn't mean that you can't play a game in a nonstandard way, but it does mean that you should consider and respect how others play the game, and you should have a good reason to play in a non-standard way when it affects others negatively. In addition, the appropriate gamer never loses sight of the fact that it is just a game. This doesn't mean that the appropriate gamer doesn't try or isn't serious, but it does mean that they will take the proper level of seriousness to the respective activity.

RAGE AND CHILLNESS

"No pestilence has been more costly for the human race [than anger]," says Seneca, the Roman Stoic. Because of its potential for destruction, Seneca called for the complete eradication of anger. In contrast, Aristotle argued there is a place for righteous anger in the good-tempered person.[16] Both, however, would agree that raging over a video game is vicious and is neither healthy for oneself nor one's community. But, alas, this is probably the most meme-able vice. There are whole YouTube series dedicated to gamers flipping out: at the less extreme end of the spectrum, the raging gamer yells; at the more extreme end, they smash their console or computer. Rage, however, isn't only directed at the inanimate, but often targets fellow players or affects other players through "rage quitting."

The virtue contrary to the vice of rage is equanimity, which is just a fancy way of saying "being chill." The person with rage is overly angry, whereas the chill person is tranquil. Whether you accept the Aristotelian position that there is proper anger or the Stoic position that anger is always bad will determine whether anger has a role in being virtuous. But both the Aristotelian and Stoic agree that we shouldn't be raging over video games and that the virtuous person will approach games with light-heartedness, joy, and calmness.

Chillness isn't just a matter of how we *act* toward others but also of how we *react*. If you play enough online games, at some point someone will disrespect you, and you have a choice of how to respond: you can blow up in rage and engage them in what will surely amount to a litany of typo-filled insults and threats ("your trash"), or you can ignore them and move on. It is a mark of distinction to respond to this disrespect in an appropriate and chill way. This isn't to say that we shouldn't report disruptive players or that we shouldn't stand up for what is right—we should do these things, but we shouldn't get caught up in immature flame wars while doing so. Marcus

Aurelius wisely tells us, "The best revenge is not to be like that."[17] Our goal, according to Marcus, is "to live life in peace, immune to all compulsion. Let them scream whatever they want." Accordingly, when we respond to toxicity, we mustn't lower ourselves, but keep a level head.

FRAGILITY AND FORTITUDE

When the going gets tough, gamers tend to quit. We aren't talking about quitting video games because you lost interest or because you have real-life responsibilities that demand your attention; we're talking about the rage-quitter who logs off mid-game out of frustration. Such gamers are displaying the vice of fragility. Though fragility can connect to rage, it is a different aspect of ethical failing. The vice of rage reflects not having the appropriate temperament, while the vice of fragility reflects not being able to endure adversity. "Cowardice" is in the neighborhood of "fragility," but it seems a bit much to say that someone is acting cowardly when they give up on a video game, though they might well be. Habitually giving up on something you desire to complete or continue to play isn't good, as it prevents you from achieving your goals and deprives you of the chance to improve. And when we become accustomed to giving up, we become quitters. Fragile gamers also let their team down in multiplayer modes—when someone quits mid-fight, the rest of the team is often left in an unwinnable position and has thus wasted their time and effort all because someone couldn't handle the in-game challenges.

However, quitting isn't the only way one can be fragile while gaming. Gamers also express fragility when they do not attempt something they want to do because they anticipate it being too difficult. This can be as simple as not trying a certain game mode that interests you because you don't want to fail, or it can involve not asking other people for help because you fear rejection.

If fragility is the vice of not being able to endure hardships, then fortitude is the associated virtue. The person with fortitude perseveres through difficult situations and overcomes adversity. In gaming, there are some truly inspiring examples of fortitude. Physical disabilities can make for a type of adversity in gaming, as games are designed with the able-bodied in mind. Despite this, there are gamers with physical disabilities who, with perseverance and ingenuity, develop ways to play. All deaf raid teams, for example, have developed ways to communicate efficiently without voice chat by using limited in-game emotes. There are gamers without hands who use foot pedals to play and quadriplegic players who control their characters by operating a joystick with their mouths. Less dramatically, when we fail and we try again, or when someone's insult doesn't prevent us from doing what we love, we take one step toward fortitude and away from fragility. In fact, a central aspect of many games involves persevering through multiple failures. The *Souls* series of games is popular in large part because of its challenging gameplay, MMO (massive multiplayer online) raid bosses can require hundreds of attempts spanning over weeks of practice before they are successfully killed, and many games include "insanity" difficulty modes. Gaming thus often offers an environment for people to express and cultivate fortitude.

DISHONESTY AND HONESTY

From lying about one's achievements to downright scamming others out of money, dishonesty has many faces in gaming. Since conning people out of money is so clearly wrong, we will talk about cheating. There are a variety of ways in

which cheating occurs in games. To name a few: some players use programs that exploit in-game mechanics, such as
programs that improve accuracy ("aimbots") or allow you to
see through walls ("wallhacks"); some players mess with the
internet or servers ("DDoSing") to their own advantage; and
some gamers exploit in-game mechanics in a way clearly not
intended by game designers (e.g., glitching into a spot where
other players can't get you). When cheating doesn't affect
(either directly or indirectly) other players (such as in single
player games) or if all parties agree upon it, then there isn't
anything necessarily wrong with it. In fact, it can be a way for
gamers to creatively explore and experiment with the game
and bond with each other over the resulting weirdness (any
kid who played Pokémon Red and Blue had a playground story to
tell about their encounter with MissingNo). However, when
all affected players have not agreed to those terms, engaging
in these practices is dishonest.

One reason cheating is dishonest is because games have
explicit cheating policies that players must agree to in order to
play the game. When cheaters violate these policies, they are
agreeing to one thing (not to cheat) and doing another (cheating). The problem is not just that the rules are being violated,
though. The deeper issue is that, in ignoring the agreed-upon
rules, the cheater will be exploiting other players to their own
advantage. Similar to the Pubstomping Tryhard, the cheater
only has an advantage if others don't cheat: if everyone were
to cheat, cheating would be pointless, as it would not give you
an edge over other players, since no one would be abiding by
the rules at all—if you ever witness two botted accounts facing each other down on the battlefield, you'll quickly realize
it is an exercise in futility.[18] Furthermore, cheating negatively
affects the gaming experience. When you cheat at a game, you

are implicitly saying that winning at the game matters more than respect for truthfulness and other players.[19] Nobody enjoys playing with cheaters, and gamers will quickly stop playing a game if cheating is prevalent.

The person who is committed to truthfulness is honest. Marcus Aurelius tells us that a "straightforward, honest person should be like someone who stinks: when you're in the same room with him, you know it."[20] Now honesty doesn't require that one always tell the truth or never tell a lie. But the stench of truthfulness must be palpable to those around. In gaming, being honest involves a serious commitment to fair play and integrity. At minimum, this requires that one should neither cheat nor benefit from another's cheating.

EGO AND HUMILITY

The sixth vice of gaming is ego. Ego is a catchall term for an inflated sense of self. The person with an ego overestimates their own gaming skills or the importance of gaming skills in life and underestimates the skills of others or the importance of other aspects of life. You might have an ego if:

- When in a team, you believe you personally deserve the majority of credit for a win.
- When in a team, you believe your teammates (rather than you) deserve the majority of blame for a loss.
- You frequently blame your losses or failures on "bugs" or "glitches" or on a faulty internet connection, rather than your own poor play.
- You believe that your video game abilities warrant you to talk down to other gamers.
- You are constantly talking about or drawing attention to yourself.

- You believe your video game abilities make you a better person than people with lesser video game abilities.
- You have a "my way or the highway" attitude toward group gameplay.
- You are a streamer, YouTuber, or NB's brother; we kid. . .kinda.

Ego is, unfortunately, quite common in gaming. Egotistical gamers often have the attitude that they can do no wrong and will constantly divert blame to others or to external circumstances, rather than owning up to their own failure. Because egotistical gamers have trouble acknowledging their own faults, they are often unable to reflect upon what they can do better to improve their performance (since, in their mind, they do everything perfect, there is nothing to improve!), and are unwilling to take any advice from others, much to the detriment of any team with which they are grouped. They may think their approach/strategy is the best one, even if the rest of the group has decided otherwise. The infamous "Leeroy Jenkins!" moment in *WoW*, when Leeroy overrides the team's discussion of strategy and charges into the group of mobs and gets his team killed, is an example.

If the egotistical person overestimates their own significance and underestimates the significance of others, then the person with humility accurately appraises themselves and others.[21] In order to achieve humility, one must follow the Delphic imperative to "know thyself." Self-knowledge, of course, requires self-reflection. However, we can't truly know ourselves without understanding others as well.[22] If we want to understand our own qualities, we need to think accurately and honestly about the character, achievements, and actions of others. This will allow us to gain a wider perspective of who we are, and what our place is, which in turn will allow us to be humble.

The humble gamer acknowledges that others around them are not just NPCs (non-playable characters) who play a supporting or thwarting role to their heroic main character; instead, they recognize that each person is the main character in their own life story and should be treated as such. The humble gamer isn't quick to blame others or to steal credit, nor do they think their gaming achievements amount to all that much in the grand scheme of things. Their ability to recognize and take responsibility for their mistakes, coupled with their recognition of the strengths of other gamers, enables the humble gamer to critically reflect on their play and take advice from others and thus become better at the game.

TOXICITY AND KINDNESS

The seventh vice of gaming is maliciousness, but because no gamer uses that word, we'll call it toxicity. By toxicity, we mean a disposition to be unnecessarily hurtful or negative to others. Toxic gamers often go out of their way to spoil the gaming experience for others, sometimes in response to what another player has done, and sometimes just because they can. Alas, there are countless ways for players to be toxic.[23] For example, players can be toxic to another gamer by saying disrespectful things to them. From the tame "Git gud scrub" to the horrible "Drink bleach," gamers are notorious for engaging in some of the lowest forms of communication. Another common toxic behavior is sabotaging. This refers to players purposely losing in order to ruin their teammates' experience. Players sometimes sabotage because they are frustrated with their teammates, and thus this vice connects to elitism, rage, fragility, and ego, but it can also occur because some players, sadly, enjoy disrupting the play of others.

Kindness is the contrary to toxicity. Following Aristotle's general account, kindness is "helpfulness toward someone in need, not in return for anything, nor for the advantage of the helper himself, but for that of the person helped."[24] Kind players go out of their way to improve the gaming experience for others without looking for anything in return. Just as there are countless ways to be toxic in gaming, there are countless ways to be kind. Kindness can be expressed in helping other players out or simply being friendly and nice.

In the *Destiny* community, more experienced gamers sometimes "sherpa" (guide) less experienced players through raids and other difficult content. In *Destiny*, many players never raid, which is unfortunate since it is some of the most dynamic, unique, and exciting content the game offers. Sherpas, thus, help break this barrier to entry. If it weren't for sherpas, who patiently and kindly kept helping NB even after his many unfortunate deaths, *Destiny* would never have become his game of choice.

We don't have to sherpa in order to be kind, though. We can show kindness simply by being compassionate and understanding to other gamers. Related to tolerance, we can recognize that we are part of a large community of people who enjoy the game differently and have their own preferences and struggles. We can even show kindness in response to toxicity, as Marcus Aurelius exhorts us to do:

> [K]indness is invincible, provided it's sincere—not ironic or an act. What can even the most vicious person do if you keep treating him with kindness and gently set him straight—if you get the chance—correcting him cheerfully at the exact moment that he's trying to do you harm.[25]

IMMODERATION AND MODERATION

The eighth vice of gaming is immoderation, which involves the excessive pursuit of pleasure. Gamers are notorious for consuming content voraciously. To non-gamers, this may sound crazy, boring, or pathetic, but when new games come out, or new content is released, gamers will take off work (or school) and play. For instance, SM has friends who will, months ahead of time, request to use their work vacation days the week when a new *WoW* expansion is released. They will then game the entire day.

The *WoW* episode of *South Park* captures an extreme version of this. After being defeated by an expert gamer who plays constantly, or as he is called in the episode, "someone with absolutely no life," the boys, with the help of Blizzard Entertainment, devise a strategy to "kill that which has no life." Defeating this expert will require a Herculean effort. Thus, the boys spend all their time playing, making their in-game characters more powerful, while their actual bodies deteriorate, becoming overweight and developing carpal tunnel, and they severely lower their standards of hygiene—at one point, Cartman continues gaming while he defecates into a bedpan held by his mom. This is not an excellent way for a human to be. If you are gaming to the point of unhealth, then you are pursuing play, pleasure, and amusement excessively. Not only is such a life unhealthy, but it also neglects virtue: someone who is only concerned with gaming can't truly be concerned with virtue, as the domain of virtue is wider than gaming.

Despite these issues, gamers might still think gaming is a fun and pleasurable experience, so gaming all day and night might seem like the perfect way to spend time. Gamers might even envy the Twitch streamers who make enough money to support a life of nonstop gaming. However, it is unclear whether the life of excessive gaming is a genuinely happy one. We'll borrow Plato's example of a leaky jar to illustrate why this is the case.[26]

Imagine you try filling up a jar that has a leak in it. As you pour water into it, water seeps from the leak—so you will need to continuously replenish your jar for it to stay full. The person who is always acting on their desires for pleasurable experiences is like a leaky jar: as soon as they satisfy one desire, another arises. Just like the leaky jar, they will need to be continuously "filled up," but with pleasurable experiences. In contrast, the moderate person's desires are balanced according to reason. They are like a jar with no leaks, so that when they satisfy a desire, they remain filled.

Who is living the happier life? The person resembling the leaky jar will never truly be satisfied, because they will constantly need to refill their jar. They will thus be in a state of constant distress, aching to satisfy a new desire. To add another analogy, being in such a state is like scratching at an itchy mosquito bite. At first, scratching feels good, but the more you scratch, the itchier it becomes, and if you keep scratching, you will soon be bleeding and in pain. This is not a happy life. The person resembling the non-leaky jar, on the other hand, is happily satisfied once they fulfill their desire, and does not face the constant need for more. Applying this idea to gaming, the person who always needs to play more will be unhappier than the person who games moderately.

We can practice moderation by taking the right attitude toward gaming consumption. This involves gaming the right amount and in the right way, which in turn involves recognizing that although gaming can have a place in our lives, it shouldn't be the only thing we focus on. Gaming shouldn't consume our lives, but should enhance them by providing an occasional way to relax, have fun, make friends, and practice virtue. We will talk more about immoderation and moderation when we discuss addiction in Chapter 4.

PUTTING IT ALL TOGETHER

Ancient virtue ethicists held that the virtues aren't isolated from each other but are interconnected.[27] Progressing or regressing with respect to one virtue affects how we fair with respect to other virtues, and together they compose your character. It would take up far too much space, and probably be a little boring, to discuss all the ways this is possible with gaming virtues, but an example will be instructive.

The humble gamer has the correct understanding of their self and others, while the egotistical gamer lacks this. As such, ego relates to gatekeeping, tryhardedness, dishonesty, and toxicity as these vices entail lacking a proper perspective of others, and humility connects to the virtues of tolerance, appropriateness, honesty, and kindness since they require it. For instance, the tolerant player considers others' perspective when they recognize that others might prefer the aspects of the game that they personally dislike. In contrast, the gatekeeper fails to consider the perspective of others when they want the game to simply fit their own vision of it. Even vices (such as, rage, fragility, immoderation) and virtues (such as, chillness, fortitude, and moderation) which might not seem connected to ego and humility can have connections. For instance, someone with an inflated ego might rage when the game doesn't go their way, while the humble person can remain chill.

Now just as we shouldn't think of the virtues and vices as being isolated from each other, we shouldn't think of our gaming self as being isolated from our overall character. There is danger in bifurcating our gaming self from our non-gaming self, as we can express excellence or deficiency through games, and how we act virtually affects others. Simply put, being an in-game jerk means that you in fact spend some of your time being a jerk—the fact that it occurs while gaming does not exonerate you. In addition, the habits we form in one specific domain (say school, games, work, etc.) are not sealed off from other domains. If we cultivate bad habits while gaming, these habits can easily spill over into other aspects of our life. After all, this is the core reason for thinking that there are activities, like music and athletics, that can cultivate character. By learning to overcome fear and struggle with adversity in a specific activity, we can apply these habits to other domains. Of course, it is possible to be more courageous in one domain than another, but our goal is to be a fully virtuous agent, which involves a commitment to virtue in all domains.[28]

Framing the ethics of gaming in terms of our character moves us beyond the narrower considerations about violence. The ethical status of gaming isn't so much a question about whether video games are ethically good or bad (though some games are best avoided), but rather a question of how one is playing the game: one's motivational state, one's emotions, and one's judgments both in the game and with respect to other players. The evidence doesn't support the claim that gaming will make us violent, but that isn't to say that it won't contribute to us being a certain type of person—be it an asshole or an angel. Gaming is a character-cultivating activity, and as such it provides the opportunity for becoming more virtuous or vicious.

KEY POINTS

- Similar to athletics, gaming can shape and reflect our character. If we play in a vicious way, not only are we acting badly, we are becoming more vicious. But if we play in a virtuous way, not only are we behaving well, we are becoming virtuous.

- In response, some might object that gaming is outside the purview of virtue and vice because it is about fun and play. In response to this, we argued that when we look at the virtue ethics tradition, we see that all activities matter ethically. Furthermore, some virtue theorists have even argued that there is a virtue of play.
- The setting of online gaming provides a unique forum to test our virtues. Like Plato's Ring of Gyges, when we game online, we are challenged to act virtuously in a scenario in which we can largely avoid the negative social repercussions of acting viciously. Accordingly, gaming offers an opportunity to develop an inherent appreciation for the virtues.
- The taxonomy of virtues and vices demonstrates various ethical dimensions in gaming, and how we can succeed and fail in each dimension. Additionally, the taxonomy can serve as a tool for reflecting on one's own gaming behavior.

Raiding, virtue, and best buds

3

> For no one would choose to live without friends even if he had all the other goods.
>
> Aristotle, *NE* 8.1.1155a5–6

SM: There is nothing quite like attending BlizzCon, the convention put on by the gaming company giant Blizzard Entertainment. It's one of the biggest video game conventions in the world, but unlike other large gaming conventions, BlizzCon is dedicated to the handful of games that Blizzard develops. This means that the attendees not only share a love of gaming, they likely share a love of playing the same games. This also means that many people travel to this specific convention to meet up with, for two days in real life (IRL), the people they regularly see in the virtual world. (For those of you who do not live part of your life in Azeroth, end-game content in *World of Warcraft* (*WoW*) centers on completing raids with a 20-person group. These raids will take the best players in the world about a week of constant play to kill all the bosses and will take lesser mortals months of bi-weekly or tri-weekly raid nights to clear. This is all to say, if you raid somewhat seriously in *WoW*, you will be spending quite a bit of time with the same 19 people.)

You might expect meeting people you have only engaged with online to be awkward (because you think they are basically strangers to you in a real-life setting), surprising (because

DOI: 10.4324/9781003308638-4

you feel it is likely they have deceived you about who they really are), or even dangerous (because you think the internet is full of predators disguising themselves as normal people in order to kidnap you—looking at you, Mom). That is to say, you might expect the people you meet up with IRL to only partially resemble the people you know in game. In reality, it's nothing like this (OK, it's a little awkward at first, but we are a group of people that spend their free time slaying bosses for loot, after all)—in fact, it's startling how much everyone is like their online selves. After the initial shock of hearing a voice you know very well being matched to a body you do not, your guildmates act just as you would expect them to, from the jokes they tell and the things they talk about to the way they handle waiting in long lines and planning out the day's activities—everything is in accordance with the personality you've come to know through gaming with them. The friendship you share with them online easily transfers to a real-life setting. SM out.

SM has no hesitation in calling her guildmates friends, even if her relationships with them take place mostly online, with the exception of the rare in-person meetup at BlizzCon. However, the idea that gamers can have real friendships with one another is controversial for two major reasons. First, there is a prevalent stereotype that gamers are anti-social losers, and the reason they are drawn to gaming in the first place is that they lack the ability to make friends IRL. Second, one might think that relationships formed through gaming (or online, in general) cannot be *real* friendships in the way that friendships IRL can be. Together, these ideas can be taken as a major reason why it's not OK to be a gamer: having real friendships contributes to living a rich and full life, so if gamers isolate themselves in the virtual world, they will be missing out on developing the skills that will allow them to make friends in person and will thus be missing out on an important good in life.

THE LONER STEREOTYPE

There's no doubt that gamers spend a lot of their time alone, strictly speaking. Gaming doesn't require one to go outside, so if you game as a hobby (in the West, at least), you are likely spending much of your time at home. PC gaming set-ups are designed with one person in mind (nostalgic old school LAN parties aside), and even though console games can be played with others in a shared space, extra controllers are an additional fee, and there are sadly very few good local co-op games. Physical isolation, therefore, appears to be the default for gamers. It's not all that surprising then that one of the associated stereotypes of the gamer is that they are loners—alone behind closed doors, cooped up in their bedrooms all day with eyes glued to the screen, forgoing real human interaction. And it's not like this stereotype doesn't bear some resemblance to the truth: hardcore gamers often prefer gaming over in-person activities—indeed, some express being "more themselves" online than in person.[1] An extreme example of this is that one of the people in SM's gaming group frequently DoorDashes Sour Patch Kids from the gas station so he doesn't have to engage with the store clerks (the DoorDasher leaves them at the door) and, for the entirety of one April, did not leave his apartment once (this was the one month the group collectively kept track). He also once casually revealed in group chat (in a tone that suggested there *was nothing weird at all about it*) that he keeps tinfoil on his windows, so he doesn't have to see the sun.

Despite the loner stereotype, a large majority of gamers report making good friends within their online gaming communities, and gamers commonly report that socializing with other players is a big part of what makes online gaming enjoyable.[2] So at the very least, most gamers are not, strictly speaking, loners in game. However, we might still worry that the social bonds formed while playing ultimately boil down to shallow interactions based on achieving in-game objectives rather than real friendships. And we might worry that, in the life of the gamer, these superficial virtual relationships end up replacing the full, rich kinds of relationships one can cultivate with others in person. That is to say, our stereotypical basement-dwelling gamer might rebuff your accusation that he is a loner by showing you his long online gaming friends list, but he could still very well be a loner in spirit because he has replaced meaningful IRL friendships based on deep mutual affection with shallow friendships online that are based on fat loot drops.

Thus, one reason video game critics may deem that the gamer lifestyle is not OK is because of what we call the "social displacement problem": the time gamers spend with their online "friends" takes over time spent cultivating IRL friendships, which is problematic because online relationships cannot provide the same kind of support and closeness that IRL relationships can.[3] Psychologist Rachel Kowert explains that, in focusing their social interactions with people online, gamers, according to the social displacement problem, "are supplanting valuable sources of social and emotional support for less intimate and diffuse online relationships."[4] Another way to think of this problem: if you eat a tub of ice cream at dinner time, you will likely be full and thus not eat the vegetable-rich dinner that your family has prepared—the ice cream has displaced your nutrition packed dinner. However, ice cream is (unfortunately) inferior to vegetables, nutrition-wise, so the displacement here is a problem with regards to your overall health. Similarly, if offline relationships are being displaced by inferior online ones, gamers will be worse off because they are missing out on making real friends.

Now that we know the problem, we can set out on trying to address it. To begin, the evidence in support of the social displacement problem is far from decisive. Some psychologists argue that, instead of displacing social relationships IRL, online relationships compensate for them. Individuals who perceive themselves as having a difficult time socializing in person see in-game relationships as an appealing alternative.[5] In addition, for many gamers, their friendship exists both in person and in game.[6] As indicated by SM's BlizzCon story, online gaming sometimes leads to in-person activity, and as will be discussed in NB's story below, online gaming is a way to sustain in-person relationships while geographically separated.

However, rather than wade through statistics and psychological evidence, which is often murky, our response to this challenge is more conceptual. If we can show that gaming friendships can be genuine friendships, then the displacement problem dissolves. Even if gamers are displacing time spent with IRL friends for time spent with online friends, this isn't necessarily a bad thing since gaming friendships are real friendships, not mere imitations. And if we can show this, then gamers aren't loners after all—destroying bosses and collecting loot doesn't preclude the cultivation of close and supportive friendships.

Before we can show that gaming friendships are real, we will first need to establish what "real" friendship means. To do this, we will introduce Aristotle's account of friendship

Image 3.1   The gamer is a social creature

and examine whether the relationships formed through gaming can meet the criteria required for real friendship.[7]

ARISTOTELIAN FRIENDSHIP IRL

Presumably, you have friends. Or, at the very least, you know people who have friends or have seen friendships depicted in movies. People generally think friendship is a good thing, and having friends is an important part of life. But what is friendship? What does it mean for someone to be your friend? What makes a relationship a friendship instead of some other kind of relationship?

Aristotle's account is useful for our purposes for three reasons. First, it is taken seriously by philosophers today as a plausible conception of friendship. Second, because of Aristotle's love of making distinctions, it is a relatively clear model, making it easy to apply. Third, it fits with the virtue-theoretic approach of the book. However, we aren't so concerned with the nitty-gritty of Aristotle's account or aspects that are culturally germane to Aristotle, but rather in how the general ideas could apply to contemporary life.

Friendship is just one of the many kinds of relationships we human beings can be involved in. These relationships can vary dramatically—the kind of relationship you have with your mother is different from the kind you have with the guy who is always working at Starbucks when you get your coffee in the morning, and both are quite different from the relationship you have with your recreational volleyball team. So, in order to understand what friendship is (and what different types of friendships there are), we might think about some of the factors that can differentiate relationships from one another more generally.

The first thing we might consider is what the goal of the relationship is. After all, there is a reason you are relating to the other person. This reason is a defining feature of the relationship, and different types of relationships can aim at different things. The goal of your relationship with the barista may be simply to get your morning coffee, and you might not really think about what the barista wants. The goal of such a relationship would thus be merely transactional, and this would not be a friendship. The goal of a used car salesman's relationship with his customers might be to make as much money as possible for himself, which might involve lying to his customers about the quality of the car. The goal of that relationship would be exploitative and clearly not friendship—as much as the salesman might try to convince you that you are buddies, he only wants to benefit himself and has no regard for your well-being.

Friendship, in contrast, involves affectionate feelings toward a friend that express caring about them for their own sake. Caring about someone for their own sake involves having goodwill towards that person—you want things to go well for them. For instance, when you hang out with your friend, you are doing so because you want to have fun with them, but you also want them to have a good time as well. In fact, your friend's enjoyment of your time together is part of why you enjoy yourself. If your friend is having a bad time, you probably will as well, and you will probably try to come up with something to do that they will enjoy more. Your enjoyment is intimately tied to your friend's enjoyment because you care about them and want them to be happy.

So, we see that friendship is distinguished from other types of relationships in that it involves friendly feelings and goodwill. Uncoincidentally, this is how Aristotle defines friendship as well. He also adds two additional conditions that he thinks are required for a friendship to count as such. One is that the relationship must be reciprocal—anyone you are friends with must also be friends with you if it's going to count as friendship. Although you might be attached to your anime body pillow and wish it well, it cannot feel the same way about you, and so it's not your friend (sorry!). The other crucial aspect of friendship, according to Aristotle, is that friends are *aware* of their mutual affection for one another. You might have, for example, two artists who follow each other's art and admire each other's work from afar, but never express this admiration to the other. Although they get pleasure from seeing each other's work and wish each other well, they are not friends since neither is aware of the other's interests.[8]

The view of friendship that we get from Aristotle, then, is that friends have mutual affection and goodwill towards each other and are aware of this mutual affection and goodwill. Because friends truly care about each other, they share pleasures and pains together. Indeed, the mere presence of a friend can inspire joy and friendly feelings.

DIFFERENT TYPES OF FRIENDSHIPS

When SM was a kid, she had several variations of "best friend" jewelry, in which one half of the jewelry said "best" and the other half said "friend," and she and her best friend each chose a half to wear (SM always chose the "best" half, for obvious reasons). It was also common for children to create ranked lists of their friends in her class. Adults don't wear such jewelry or create such lists (and if they do, they probably shouldn't), but we all have an implicit idea that some of our friends are closer to us than others. You might have 500-plus people labeled as "friends" on your social media account, but your "friendship" with many of these people is quite a bit different from the friendship you share with the person you'd feel comfortable calling for help in the middle of the night when you are sick with food poisoning. There are different types of friendship that correspond to different levels of depth, or closeness, that friendship can have. Once again, Aristotle can help us understand what differentiates these different types of friendships.

Though there is some amount of friendly feeling and good-will in all friendships, friendships can be based on different qualities and occur in different contexts. Friendship, Aristotle reasoned, can be based on (1) usefulness, (2) pleasure, or (3) goodness. Friendship of goodness is really friendship of character and virtue since what we love about another person is their virtuous character. The perfect form of friendship is based on goodness, and this form of friendship sets the standard by which friendship is measured—the other friendships are friendships merely by how they resemble the friendship of goodness.[9]

To help clarify, let's consider three sample cases of friends. Friend 1 is Aly, who you met in your biology class. By chance, you chose seats next to each other at the start of the semester. The course is tough, but you want to do well in it, and you know you do better learning material when you have a study partner. You've noticed that Aly always attends class, is attentive, and takes copious notes (you've also noticed that she rarely watches random videos on her laptop during class like almost everyone else does). You also do your best to be a good student in the class, so you figure Aly would be a good study buddy for you. You ask her if she wants to prep for the first test with you, and she agrees. You both have a productive study session and feel you've helped each other master the content for the first test, so you continue to study together for the rest of the semester. Most of your time together is spent helping each other learn the course material, but you occasionally share personal information and crack jokes. You sincerely care about Aly, and she sincerely cares about you, but the relationship revolves around schoolwork and doesn't exist outside this context.

Friend 2 is Brice, who lives down the hall from you. One day you see him wearing a shirt with a character from an anime you like on it, so you start talking to him about it. It turns out you both like watching similar genres of anime. You and Brice start hanging out and watching new shows together. The time you spend together usually revolves around your shared interest—watching or talking about shows and occasionally going to local conventions together. You have a blast with Brice and love talking about anime with him, but you have no other context for your shared relationship.

Friend 3 is Anna, who you've known for many years. You hang out with her often, doing all kinds of activities together—some of the things you enjoy more, and some of the things she enjoys more. You and Anna know each other's life stories well, and she is one of the first people you think to tell about the good things that happen in your life (and she to you) because you know she will be just as happy and excited for you as you are yourself. She's also the person you go to when you need advice or just need to talk because you know not only that she will be there for you, but also that she will tell you (gently and supportively) what you can improve on. She can see the best version of you even when you can't and can get you back on the right track when you feel lost. You'd do all the same for her because she's truly a great person, and you want her to live the best life possible (and you'd be happy to split a piece of "best friend" jewelry with her).

Each friend above reflects one of the three bases for Aristotelian friendships—use, pleasure, and goodness. With our three friends in mind, we can see that friendships based on usefulness or pleasure are based on things other than the other person (they are extrinsic, as the philosophers say), in a way that friendship based on goodness is not. You are friends with Aly because you both need to study, and you are friends with Brice because you both like anime, but you are friends with Anna simply because she is Anna. Yes, you and Anna are useful to each other and enjoy doing things together, but ultimately you have remained friends for so long because of the person that she is. Friendship of use or pleasure depends on each person continuing to find each other useful or pleasant, but circumstances and tastes often change. When the biology course is over, your friendship with Aly is likely to dissolve because you are no longer of use to one another. Similarly, if Brice loses interest in anime, you will lose the thing that connects you to him, and the friendship will likely not last. Your friendship with Anna, however, does not depend on anything external to Anna herself. As long as Anna remains Anna, your friendship will persist.[10]

Character friendships, like the friendship you have with Anna, are the purest form of friendship because the friendship is primarily based in who each friend is—which means that it involves the most loving of each other for each other's own sake. When friendship is based on the character of the friend, your feelings about that friend are based on, to use a common phrase, *who they are on the inside*. This means that friendships of character are also more stable and consistent than the other types of friendships because your friends' overall personality and character will likely remain largely the same over time, even if their tastes and circumstances change. And, it gets even better: because your friends of character will also be useful and enjoyable, virtue friendships include the goods of the other two types of friendship.

Character friendships thus require that your relationship with your friend be based on your love for their character. But note that this requires that your friend (and you, yourself, since your friend must also love your character) has a loveable character, which means that you must both have virtuous character traits like honesty, kindness, practical wisdom, etc. This requirement actually makes quite a bit of sense when you think about it, given the inevitable fact that life is hard, and we will all face difficult situations that can test our friendship. If friends lack sound character, these situations can easily cause a friendship to unravel. The Stoic philosopher Epictetus gives us an excellent example of this: "No doubt you've seen dogs playing with, and fawning before, each other, and thought, 'Nothing could be friendlier.' But just throw some meat in the middle, and then you'll know what friendship amounts to."[11] Epictetus' point is that if friends do not have good character (little dogs do not), their relationship can easily turn sour under difficult conditions. The movie *Mean Girls* also illustrates this point well: although the girls claim to be best friends, their jealousy, pettiness, and narcissism cause their friendships to be torn apart over trivial things like who got nominated for Spring Fling Queen and who got candy canes from whom.

Because the friends in a virtue friendship have good character, an important additional benefit of virtue friendships is that they can help us develop our own character: as Aristotle states, friends become "better from their activities and their mutual correction. For each molds the other in what they approve of, so that, as the saying goes, 'you will learn what is noble from noble people.'"[12] We can see the good in our friends, and use that as a model for our own future behaviors, and our friends can help correct us when they see we are not being our best selves. Virtue friends can thus inspire each other to be their best selves.

Just like the best loot drops, friendships of virtue are rare.[13] Not only do they require that the people involved be virtuous—something itself rare—they also require a great deal of time so that friends can get to know each other's character and develop trust in each other. Indeed, the relationship should evolve into friends "living together"—sharing their lives by hanging out and pursuing their life projects together. Aristotle provides us with some examples of such pleasant pursuits: drinking, playing dice, doing gymnastics, and doing philosophy.[14] In addition to the basic conception of living together as doing activities, Aristotle also has a special sense of living together as "sharing in perception."[15] The idea of "sharing perception" is connected to Aristotle's idea of "a friend as another self."[16] The attitudes that we have toward our friends derive from our attitudes toward ourselves: just as we want to be happy, we wish our friends to be happy. We also share in their joy and pain, as if it were happening to ourselves—when your friend gets the job they really wanted, for example, you feel that happiness with them.[17] Because of these shared perceptions, we see ourselves in our friends. But, according to Aristotle, the core, essential aspect of each person is our *rational self*: our reflective thoughts, attitudes, and decisions—what makes you *you* are not just the things you like and dislike, but the way you *think* about things, the way you *reason*. This means that what counts as living together is, according to Aristotle, "the sharing of conversation and thought, not sharing the same pasture, as in the case of grazing animals."[18]

Thus, to truly live together in a human way isn't merely to spend one's time stuffing one's face and guzzling drink with associates near you—that is for the cows—but involves having intellectual conversations together. This allows us to not only come to know the rational aspects—including the good character—of our friends that are essential to who they are as people, but it also is a unique type of pleasurable experience because we are able to see our own rational selves, our own good character, reflected in our friends. A good person will find pleasure in what their virtuous friends do both because these actions are good (since a virtuous person is doing them) and because they can see their own excellence reflected in their friend's actions—something they can't do on their own.[19] So besides having a wonderful person to inspire us and to have joy with, a virtuous friend can actually teach us about ourselves, and this experience is uniquely pleasant. No wonder such relationships are rare: besides demanding the virtues, these relationships require intimacy and transparency, and such commitments, according to Aristotle, make it impossible to have many friendships of virtue.

GAMING FRIENDSHIPS AS FRIENDSHIPS OF PLEASURE AND USE

Let's begin by distinguishing between social interactions and friendships in gaming. Many of the most popular games today involve an online multiplayer component. Such games are social in the sense that you will encounter others who are in the gaming world at the same time you are. However, most encounters with other people while online gaming, just like most encounters with other people IRL, will be mere social interactions. This can be as simple and mundane as hanging out in the same capital city with other players, or it can be more complicated and intense such as taking down a boss together or battling it out in PvP. Though these interactions have value, they are brief and anonymous affairs and thus cannot be friendships because they lack the mutually acknowledged reciprocal goodwill found in friendship. These virtual interactions are akin to the IRL interactions one has at the grocery store or driving: they remind us that we are not alone in the world, that others are sharing the space with us going about their own business, but this alone is not sufficient for friendship.

Sometimes, though, our encounters with others in the gaming world are not brief and anonymous. Many gamers (ourselves included) have a group of people they enjoy playing with and play with regularly, scheduling times to specifically play together in much the same way that people IRL schedule times to hang out with the people they enjoy hanging out with. To help understand these more involved and consistent relationships, recall from the above discussion that there are three main types of friendship, each based on a different reason for loving a friend—their usefulness, the pleasurable experiences you have with them, or the goodness of their character.

Given these three types of friendships, friendships of pleasure seem to be the most common for gaming friendships: gaming is, after all, mostly a source of leisure and entertainment, and thus friends that game together are likely to have a relationship that is based on their enjoyment of the games they play. Gaming friendships that begin with gamers playing the same game and finding that they enjoy playing together are likely to be friendships of pleasure. Such friends might schedule time to play games together and will probably use voice chat to talk about what is going on in the game and to casually chat about non-game things. If a gaming friend expresses that they don't enjoy doing a certain in-game activity, then the other friend will avoid making that friend do that thing since both friends want each other to enjoy their time playing together. However, if gaming friends lose interest in the games they share an interest in, they will likely lose touch with one another. The reciprocal concern for each other's enjoyment along with the dependence of the relationship on a shared interest in gaming exemplify the qualities of friendships of pleasure.

However, there may also be friendships in gaming that are better categorized as friendships of use. In multiplayer games, one often must rely on the skills of their other teammates to succeed. Such conditions can lead to gaming friendships that are based more on the reciprocal usefulness of the team members rather than shared enjoyment of the game. Friendships of use are common in MMO games that require relatively large but stable groups of people to cooperate and fulfill specific in-game roles. For example, in *WoW*, the hardest level of content, mythic raiding, requires a group of 20 people. Defeating raid bosses at this difficulty level requires a lot of practice learning the fights—boss encounters may take hundreds of failed attempts before they are successfully killed. Because of this, the raid group of 20 needs to be consistent across the weeks of play it might take to defeat a boss. Within the raid group, several different roles need to be fulfilled as well, and so each person in the group needs to be able to successfully perform their specific role. Though there is mutual goodwill, and though the activity is leisurely, the relationship depends on use: if a raid member decides they want to stop high-level raiding, or if they decide they want to switch roles to something that the raid group does not need, then the friendship often dissolves. These qualities are indicative of a friendship of use.

Although these types of friendships are imperfect, they shouldn't be dismissed as insignificant. A study buddy is a friendship of use, but they can bring much-needed respite from tedious and challenging coursework. They can even make both parties look forward to a class they wouldn't otherwise enjoy. Friendships of pleasure, in particular, contribute to a rich and meaningful life, as they allow one to share enjoyment with another person ("double the pleasure, double the fun," as the wisdom of commercial advertisements teaches us). Thus, even if gaming friendships could only reach the level of friendships of pleasure—and it seems clear that they can—this would be enough to demonstrate that gaming affords the opportunity to develop meaningful friendships, and thus enough to show that gamers need not be anti-social. There are plenty of opportunities in all kinds of multiplayer games to develop friendships of use and pleasure.

That being said, gamers love a challenge and are completionists by nature, and so you might be wondering if gaming relationships can beat the highest difficulty mode: friendship of virtue. We thus now turn to the more complicated and important question of whether gaming relationships can be the best type of friendship: friendship that can help us develop and understand our own virtuous character. To make this case, we'll first explain how gaming friendships can enhance and sustain IRL friendships, then we'll move on to purely virtual friendships.

SUSTAINING FRIENDSHIPS THROUGH GAMING

If you've ever played *Oregon Trail*, you know that people in the past used to stay put for the most part, since long-distance traveling posed a significant risk of death by dysentery or trying to ford a river too deep. But now, with planes, trains, and the best job and educational opportunities not always being in your hometown, it is increasingly common for people to make geographically large moves throughout their lifetime. Sadly, such moves require that we leave behind our friends, and even the best friendships are difficult to maintain under these conditions. Aristotle himself notes that "distance does not dissolve the friendship unqualifiedly, but only its activity. But if the absence is long, it also seems to cause the friendship to be forgotten."[20] In other words, when you stop interacting with your friend regularly, it is difficult to continue the kind of living together with your friend that virtue friendship requires, and even those of us with the best intentions for remaining friends can find ourselves in the situations where we only think of our distant friend when social media reminds us that it is their birthday. However, online gaming can be a way of continuing in-person relationships when people are separated geographically. Many parents were thankful that gaming allowed their children to continue their relationships with their friends during COVID lockdowns, and for one of us, gaming has provided a continued way of maintaining an important friendship.

NB: I didn't really get into games until I was an adult. I grew up playing Nintendo, Sega Genesis, and N64 with my brother, but being the little brother, I spent more time watching than playing. However, when I moved away for college, I stopped playing regularly. When I got my first academic job, my brother asked me to get a PS4 so that we could play together. In my head, I quickly dismissed this idea since I wasn't that into gaming, and spending money on a source of entertainment that collected dust wasn't something I was interested in doing. The more I thought about it, the more I realized that this wasn't really about gaming but about spending time with my brother, which was well worth the cost of the console. So I bought it and soon came to appreciate and enjoy gaming—hence this book. But in addition to this, I also started to regularly hang out with my brother. Before video games, I only spent time with my brother when I saw him in person, which was major holidays and the occasional summer visit. But with video games, I hang out with him at least three times a week while gaming. I use the phrase "hang out" with my brother rather than "talk to" since we are engaged in a shared activity together.[21] Some of our hanging out involves shared projects in the Destiny universe, but some also involves talking about family and work. We share in joy, laughter, frustration, and we even get in childlike disputes concerning the game. Our gaming friendship has been a source of joy and fun in my life, and I often look forward to our gaming sessions while at work. NB out.

NB and his brother don't meet Aristotle's standard of virtue.[22] Few do. Despite this, it makes sense to classify this as a virtue friendship since the basis of the friendship is neither pleasure nor use; the whole point of playing was so that they could continue their life together through a shared activity. In addition, both NB and his brother aspire to help each other be better people. When personal conflicts or hardships arise, they talk through them and try to figure out what is best.[23]

THE FINAL BOSS: VIRTUAL VIRTUE FRIENDSHIPS

Online gaming can thus be a way of living together with the virtue friends we already have. What is more debatable, however, is whether a virtue friendship can take place entirely online. In a special issue of the journal Ethics and Information Technology—one of the main ethics and technology journals— philosophers examined online friendships from an Aristotelian perspective.[24] Most philosophers argued that virtue friendships couldn't occur in a purely virtual medium, but conceded that friendships of pleasure and virtue that had a real-life component could be developed and sustained online.[25] Much of the target of the debate was social media, but some of the arguments also applied to virtual gaming relationships. Though the objections were varied, they converged on the main point that in online relationships, the character of the other person is not transparent.[26]

In person, our friends can experience first-hand how we behave in a given situation. If we truly share our life with another person, as virtue friendship requires, then we can't choose which aspects of ourselves to show since our friend will be along for the ride witnessing it. In contrast, the nature of online relationships precludes this level of transparency. These authors argue that friends can intentionally only show certain aspects of themselves in online relationships. Moreover, the limited range of interactions available online restricts how well we can really know each other. Hence, even if friends wanted to be fully transparent, they couldn't since, unlike in-person interactions which are often varied and random, online interactions are limited. Call this objection: the "transparency objection." In order to establish that gaming friendships can be virtue friendships, we will need to overcome it.

First, though it is true that online interactions give us more control and thus more opportunities to be less transparent than in-person interactions, it's not as though real-life interactions are fully transparent either.[27] We do have quite a bit of control over how we present ourselves in person: someone might wear Supreme clothing because they want to appear rich and cool to others, while someone else might put activist stickers all over their laptop because they want to appear compassionate and tolerant, and someone else might drive a huge lifted truck because they want to appear to be tough and macho. However, these appearances can disguise our true character, and all too often, the people that try hardest to appear a certain way are not really that way at all.

Furthermore, most in-person interactions don't begin with full transparency anyway. It is unlikely an ex-convict leads with their criminal past when meeting new people and friends, nor is it likely that someone discloses their personal reflections on the meaning of life to the people they just met at the running club. It is only after we get more comfortable and gain each other's trust that we begin to share more personal details about our deeply held beliefs, our pasts, and our hopes for the future. This is why Aristotle, who only had in-person relationships in mind, maintained that really getting to know another person required a great deal of time and effort. So, while "catfishing" occurs mostly online, we should be careful to think of our in-person interactions as entirely transparent. Online relationships might start out as slightly less transparent than real-life relationships, but there is no reason to think that online friendships cannot become more transparent with time and effort, just as real-life friendships can.

Second, gaming does in fact reveal our character to our gaming friends.[28] In Chapter 2, we argued that gaming, like athletics, is a character-cultivating activity—you can game in a way that promotes virtue or vice. When we are deeply immersed in an activity, we become more transparent because we become lost in the moment; rather than having the space to plan how to present ourselves to others, we just are. Just as we can become lost in a moment when trying to make a game-winning shot in basketball, we can get lost in a moment in a heated game of PvP or trying to destroy a final boss. Thus, friends who routinely play with each other will come to know each other's character. You might not know a person's height, weight, race, or sex, but you will know if they rage out when you fail, gloat during victory, persevere when the going gets tough or quit. And with our close gaming friends, we can work on improving our shortcomings.[29] For example, one friend might gently note that the other gets excessively angry after sustaining multiple in-game failures. Because the angry friend knows that this comment comes from a place of genuine friendship, the angry friend can use this to reflect on the way they reacted while playing, and perhaps even more generally in other situations in life. Therefore, close and regular gaming friendships reveal our character.

In fact, gaming friendships can sometimes allow for more transparency than IRL friendships. It can do so in two ways: first, gaming might provide an environment that allows people to evaluate character in the absence of potential biases, and second, it allows some people to display their character to a greater extent than they can IRL.

First, when evaluating the overall character of a person, evaluators are often biased by various irrelevant physical traits such as height, weight, race, facial symmetry, able-bodiedness, etc. The infamous halo effect bias is an example of this: the overall physical attractiveness of a person can alter how others judge their non-physical characteristics, like intelligence, competence, kindness, etc. People who are rated more physically attractive tend to be rated higher on all other good qualities as well (the halo effect's negative partner, the horn effect, causes the opposite effect). These biases can obscure our real selves, painting us in more positive or negative lights simply based on physical details that are irrelevant to our character traits. Accordingly, removing them in a virtual setting can provide a kind of honesty that isn't available in person.[30]

Second, there are various conditions that can make it difficult to interact with others in person. Someone with social anxiety might find it difficult to really "be themselves" around others in person because they will be overwhelmed with concern over how others are perceiving them and various other aspects of the environment that they cannot control. Someone with physical disabilities might find it difficult to fully engage in "normal" social activities in person and might find that it is difficult for people they meet IRL to "see past" their disability. Freed from the in-person conditions that can provoke anxiety or restrict what one can do physically, some people might find themselves able to interact with others more openly and genuinely, allowing their personality to shine through.[31] In fact, one strategy clinical psychologist (and gamer) Alexander Kriss takes for improving patients' in-person social skills is to work with them on expanding their in-game personality to outside the game. Kriss maintains that some of his patients' healthiest and most authentic self is their in-game self, and for these patients it makes more sense to work on expressing their in-game characteristics in person rather than weaning them off games.[32] Hence, sometimes gaming relationships can show who we are at a deeper level than in-person interactions can, and thus they can be an excellent medium for developing a virtue friendship.

Now one might concede that gaming friendships can show our character, but they might still worry that they can't constitute sharing life together since they just involve one domain of life—so we still aren't seeing each other fully in gaming friendships. Although players may begin their friendship as a friendship of pleasure that revolves around enjoying the game together, there is ample opportunity while playing to get to know more about who the person is outside of the game.

Gamers today also frequently use applications that allow for both voice and text chat, and conversations between gaming friends are often constantly ongoing throughout the day on these platforms, furthering the ability for gaming friends to share their lives outside the game with one another. We both have, for instance, helped our gaming friends with résumés and personal statements, among other things, and with our closer gaming friends, we have had more serious and personal discussions. In a purely online setting, gaming friends can work on their character together, witness each other act well or poorly, share their thoughts and feelings about their in-person experiences, and reflect together about life and its meaning. Using Aristotle's general criteria, this constitutes sharing a life together. Of course, these online friendships might be rare, difficult, and take a great deal of time, but that is also true of in-person relationships.

THE ADVANTAGES OF GAMING FRIENDSHIP

Friendship is an essential part of a good life. As Aristotle notes in the epigraph above, friends make life worth living. Some people worry that gaming hinders the development of friendship, replacing deep personal relationships with shallow imitations. Using an Aristotelian account of friendship, we responded to this worry by arguing that gaming relationships can be real friendships. For Aristotle, there are friendships of use, pleasure, and virtue, with virtue being the best type. Most gaming friendships will be friendships of pleasure, but we have argued that gaming friendships can be virtue friendships. Through gaming, we can sustain in-person virtue friendships when not in proximity and can also develop entirely online virtue friendships. Furthermore, as SM's BlizzCon's story illustrates, gaming friendships that begin entirely online can develop into in-person relationships—indeed, there are many stories of people finding their significant other through gaming.

Being a gamer also provides a great medium for meeting new friends. As we get older, it can be hard to make friends. Multiple factors can contribute to this: we sometimes move to places where we don't know anyone, we are no longer surrounded by individuals in our age range as we would be in school, and we become busy with our career and family. We can, of course, develop friendships at work or with our new neighbors, but these people will tend to have similar backgrounds as us. For example, people who live on the same block tend to have roughly the same social-economic status, and people at the same job tend to have the same educational background. Gaming's reach is wider and more diverse. Just as athletics can bring together people from different backgrounds and provide a source of unification and social progress, so can gaming. Through games, we can develop friends with people from a wide range of backgrounds, which can provide us with a broader perspective of the world. And because gamers already have a shared interest in something, despite differences in background, friendly feelings and affection arise naturally. From this friendship, a sense of cosmopolitan community can develop. As Seneca writes

> Friendship creates between us shared interest that includes everything. Neither good times nor bad affect just one of us; we live in common. And no one can have a happy life if he looks only to himself, turning everything to his own advantage. If you want to live for yourself, you must live

for another. This sense of companionship links all human beings to one another; it holds that there is a common law also of humankind.[33]

Thus, gaming, at its best, can not only forge bonds of friendship, but can also connect and unify diverse groups of people. But, alas, gaming isn't always at its best: it can be shallow and toxic. However, these failings do not show that being a gamer isn't OK, they merely show that one should not be a shallow and toxic person.

KEY POINTS

- The social displacement problem is the concern that gamers displace genuine in-person friendships with superficial in-game relationships.
- For Aristotle, there are three types of friendships: friendships of use; friendships of pleasure; and friendships of virtue, which is the best.
- Some philosophers worry that gaming can only achieve friendship of use or pleasure, but not friendships of virtue because of the lack of transparency in virtual mediums. This is the transparency objection.
- Our response to the transparency objection is that: (a) we should be cautious about overstating how transparent in-person relationships are; (b) gaming friendships demonstrate our character—in fact, they can sometimes demonstrate our character more than in-person relationships—; and (c) gaming friendships can go beyond merely gaming together and include other aspects of life.
- Our response to the social displacement problem is that gaming friendships can be genuine friendships. So rather than worrying about whether in-game relationships replace

in-person relationships, we should instead focus on developing genuine friendships, which are possible both in and out of games.

- Ultimately, though, we aren't forced to choose between in-person friendships and in-game friendships: for many gamers, there is both an in-person and an in-game component to the friendship.

Hooked on gaming

4

They left at once and soon met the Lotus-eaters, who had no intention of harming my companions but gave them the honey-sweet fruit of the lotus to eat. And those who ate of the fruit lost all desire to come back; the only thing that they wanted was to stay with the Lotus-eaters and feed on the fruit and never go home again.

Odysseus, *Odyssey* 9.89–95

SM: When *Diablo III* (D3) first came out in 2012 it was, for lack of better phrase, a pile of crap. The highly anticipated game turned out to be such a huge disappointment that most people, including me and my gaming friends, stopped playing it soon after it came out. I uninstalled the game and pretty much forgot it existed . . . until nearly two years later, when the *Reaper of Souls* (RoS) expansion was released. RoS completely revamped D3's end game by adding the extremely replayable Adventure Mode. And when I say "extremely replayable" I mean "find it difficult to stop playing enough to fulfill my basic life responsibilities." Yes, I was hooked. Adventure Mode basically involves two activities: completing Bounties which award various crafting mats and loot and running Nephalem Rifts, which drop random loot along the way and allow for increasing difficulty levels. Although this might not sound exciting, the hack and slash format is plain fun and the fast-paced gameplay style and loot system, along with the public leaderboards for rift completion, form the perfect recipe

DOI: 10.4324/9781003308638-5

for an addictive gaming experience. The bright flashing spell effects and randomized loot drops are reminiscent of casino slot machines, and there is a system in place for literal loot gambling with in-game currency.

I (and many other players) ended up trapped in a cycle of pushing Greater Rift levels to get gear, and getting better gear so I could push higher Rift levels. I was having fun, but there was also the sense that I had a thirst for better gear that I couldn't quite quench. RoS's release happened to coincide with a difficult time in my life: I was at the point in my PhD program where I needed to pick a topic for my dissertation but had no idea what I was going to pick. I was also feeling like I sucked at philosophy compared to everyone else and was overall uncertain about the direction I wanted my life to go. I didn't want to think about these problems—I wanted to push Greater Rifts. And so I did—to the further detriment of my schoolwork. I eventually got over my D3 obsession (the game does get boring once you've gotten the best gear) and managed to get back on track in grad school, but the whole experience demonstrated to me how easy it is to use video games to escape from life's problems. SM out

There's no doubt that video games have the power to pull us in; it is all too easy to start gaming and suddenly look out at the window and realize hours have passed without you being aware of it. Excessive gaming seems to be much more than just an occasional occurrence for many players, and parents are repeatedly warned by daytime television that their children are at risk of video game addiction. But the idea that video games are addictive isn't just something worried parent groups share on social media—like the connection between gaming and aggression, worries about gaming addiction have received quite a bit of scientific credibility. In scientific literature, video games have been compared to heroin and other drugs in terms of their addictive potential—in fact, the increasing occurrence of problematic gaming behavior has led to Internet Gaming Disorder (IGD) being included in the recent editions of the World Health Organization's International Classification of Diseases and in the American Psychiatric Association's (APA's) *Diagnostic and Statistical Manual of Mental Disorders* (DSM).[1] Add to this the handful of tragic deaths linked to excessive play that have drawn media attention—young males collapsing after days-long gaming sessions in internet cafes, and babies dying from neglect while their parents are absorbed in a game—and it's not surprising that the addictive nature of video games has become a primary reason why being a gamer is thought to not be OK.[2] If gaming is on par with illegal substances known for ruining the quality of one's life, then perhaps we really should just say no to video games. However, before we "stomp out" video games or assign them a special ribbon color, we need to get a better idea of what addiction means.

GAMING ADDICTION: LEGITIMATE DISORDER OR EPISTEMIC DUMPSTER FIRE?

The term "addiction" gets thrown around quite a bit in casual discourse—it's not unusual for people to describe things they like a lot as "addictive." Your friend might see you walk into work with your third pumpkin spice latte of the day and say something like, "You're really addicted to those things!" and you might include that you are "addicted to rock climbing" on your online dating profile, but these things are not really addictions. SM's mom recently declared she was "getting addicted to these Thai noodle bowls" after ordering her second one from the local vegan place in the same number of weeks, but SM did not take this as a cry for help over her mom's inability to stop ordering noodle bowls and the life-destroying properties of their peanut sauce, but rather as an expression of her enjoyment of the dish. We take it that when people are worried about the addictive nature of video games, they are worried about addiction in the clinical or "real" sense, rather than in the "casual conversation" sense.

Clinical addiction is a diagnosable mental disorder: if video games really are addictive, then gamers could be diagnosed with (and treated for) gaming addiction, just as drug users can be diagnosed with (and treated for) substance addiction. So, when we are answering the question of whether video games are addictive, we are thus answering the question of whether gaming addiction should count as a clinical mental disorder. The answer that the community of mental health professionals seems on the verge of giving is, yes, gaming addiction is a real mental disorder, similar to drug and gambling addiction. IGD can now be found among lists of diagnosable mental disorders, and if you do an internet search for "gaming addiction," you will find many licensed therapists and addiction clinics eager to help you overcome your problematic relationship with video games—for a fee, of course.

However, many researchers disagree with the idea that excessive gaming should really count as an addiction. Although they recognize that excessive gaming can be problematic, they do not view this problem as one that resembles other diagnosable addictions, and do not think there is enough scientific or clinical evidence to support the claim that problematic gaming is an addiction. As one of these objectors has succinctly put it, gaming is "absolutely not an addiction" and pathologizing it in this way is an "epistemic dumpster fire."[3]

How can it be that a mental disorder can occupy the space in limbo between scientifically accepted illness and the aforementioned "epistemic dumpster fire"? Well, this is because the set of things that are considered mental disorders—a set that is "officially" collected and maintained in the DSM—changes over time. Among the changes from DSM-*IV* to DSM-*V* was a substantial change to the addiction category: the DSM-*V* revamped the Substance-Related Disorders category found in the previous version to the broader Substance-Related and Addictive Disorders category. This change reflected a significant shift in the field's concept of addiction: no longer was addiction primarily thought of as a disease of physiological dependency on a substance; instead, it was replaced with the idea that addiction involves "compulsive" engagement with a rewarding stimulus, resulting in negative consequences. With this shift came the idea that not just drugs, but also certain *activities* and *behaviors* can be addictive. Gambling, which had been found in previous versions of the DSM under a different category, was a clear fit for the new addiction section under the new understanding of addiction and was accordingly moved there. However, gambling is not the only behavior that we often think of as being addictive, and it was not the only behavior considered for the new addiction section. Sex, work, eating, exercise, shopping, and playing video games are also behaviors that are rather commonly described as being addictive. All these behaviors were considered for inclusion as well, but only gaming was deemed to have a large enough body of existing research supporting both the claim that gaming has addictive properties and the claim that video game addiction has demonstrably negative consequences associated with it. In regards to the former claim, the APA points to evidence showing that "gaming prompts a neurological response that influences feelings of pleasure and reward, and the result, in the extreme, is manifested as addictive behavior," while in regards to the latter, they hold that "the 'gamers' play compulsively, to the exclusion of other interests . . . result[ing] in clinically significant impairment or distress."[4] Thus, only gaming received the hallowed honor of joining gambling as an official addictive behavior.

Well, *almost* official: IGD is currently found in the DSM's "Conditions for Further Study" section. Psychologists have reason to think IGD is a real disorder, but they need more research to establish what diagnosing it and treating it will involve. By including a preliminary definition of the disorder for further study, researchers now have a better idea of what they are researching, and data on IGD can be gathered in a more uniform way. But importantly, by including IGD in the "Conditions for Further Study" section, psychologists are saying that they have reason to think IGD is a real disorder, and by modelling its diagnosis off of addiction, they are saying that they believe it resembles other addictive disorders in its symptoms, causes, and treatments.

HOW SHALL I COMPARE THEE?

Now that we know IGD's current status as a disorder, let's take a look at its diagnostic criteria, which are essentially the same as those for substance use and gambling disorders—the other disorders in the broader "addiction" category.[5] Feel free to assess yourself as you read along![6]

(1) Preoccupation: you spend a lot of time thinking about gaming or planning when you can play again.
(2) Withdrawal: you experience unpleasant symptoms when you can't game.
(3) Tolerance: you need to spend increasing amounts of time engaged in games, play more exciting games, and/or purchase more powerful equipment to get the desired effect.

(4) Loss of control: you have tried to reduce the amount you play but have been unsuccessful in doing so.

(5) Give up other activities: you have lost interest or reduced participation in other hobbies and entertainment because of gaming.

(6) Continue despite problems: you continue gaming despite being aware of negative consequences it is causing you like neglecting important duties, losing sleep, being late to work, etc.

(7) Deception: you lie about or try to hide how much you game.

(8) Escape: you use games to forget about personal problems or relieve negative moods.

(9) Negative consequences: you risk losing significant relationships and opportunities because of gaming.

If you experienced five or more of the above symptoms within the past year, then you're a video game addict, at least according to the DSM-V criteria. Are you worried? Don't shell out the $27 for GameQuitters.com's online program just yet. If you identify as a gamer and consider gaming one of your main hobbies, then it is rather likely you count as an addict, as several of the criteria are trivially easy to meet. The "preoccupation" and "give up other activities" criteria, for example, are simply things that happen when anyone gets really into any hobby: when you find something you really enjoy spending your free time on, you will likely spend a lot of time thinking about it and looking forward to when you can do it again, and as a result, you will spend less time on other hobbies. No one would bat an eye if you replaced video games with cooking or rock climbing as the hobby you were into, so it is hard to see how these criteria would be indicative of anything pathological.

The "escape" criterion is similarly benign: people often use the hobbies they enjoy to feel better. After having a crappy day, getting into a dungeon group and joining your friends on voice chat can really help calm you down and improve your mood. In fact, when compared to its other addictive bedfellows (alcohol, drugs, gambling, etc.), gaming seems like a much better "escape," as it can relieve stress, focus one's mind toward goals, and provide a venue for making friends, all without the accompanying destructive behaviors. We'll have more to say about this in the next section—stay tuned, kids!

Generally speaking, lying is bad, and thus lying about gaming is problematic. But the relevant issue at stake in this chapter is whether the lying is indicative of addiction, and the answer is unclear. The lying could stem from someone's inability to control how much they game, or because they are aware that it negatively affects their life and don't want others to know how bad it is, or it could simply be a matter of saving social face. Playing video games is still perceived as a childish pastime (see Chapter 5), and people rarely include "spends an hour a night gaming" on their online dating profiles if they are trying to cast a wide net (and, from our experience, there is something awkward about telling an established academic who works on "serious" stuff that you are currently writing a book about video games). So, there are reasons other than addiction why one might lie or not disclose the extent to which one games.

The "withdrawal" and "tolerance" criteria have a rather awkward connection to gaming. Withdrawal and tolerance have long been associated with substance addictions. Prior to the inclusion of behavioral addictions into the addiction framework, they were historically thought of as physiological effects an addictive substance has on the body as a result of repeated use. The basic idea is that drugs are chemicals that have a biological effect on our bodies, and after recurrent use, the body "gets used to" having a certain amount of that chemical in it—having so much of that chemical become a baseline state for the body, and this is accompanied by various biological changes. Withdrawal refers to the symptoms that occur when someone stops the thing they are addicted to. When it comes to substance addiction, the body has gotten used to having a certain level of the substance in the body, so when that level decreases, the body must biologically adjust to the new level, a process that, to put it simply, does not feel good.

Tolerance refers to the reduced response to a substance following repeated use, causing a user to need increasing amounts of a substance (more doses) in order to achieve the same effects as before. Again, this has historically been a physiological concept: the body biologically adapts to having the substance in the body, and so more is needed to get above the baseline state. When it comes to trying to translate these traditionally physiological notions to behavioral addictions, the concepts become fuzzier. Behaviors do not directly alter the body's baseline levels of chemicals like substances do, and so it makes little sense to define withdrawal and tolerance on a physiological basis when it comes to behavioral addictions. Withdrawal in IGD is thus defined primarily by emotional states: feeling anxious, sad, irritable, etc. after one has stopped gaming. Tolerance in IGD gets defined in terms of time spent playing and investment in gaming equipment.

When it comes to drug addiction, both withdrawal and tolerance are not only symptoms of drug addiction, but also as part of the explanation for addictive behaviors, like continuing to use despite the negative consequences. The negative experience of withdrawal symptoms in substance addictions is one reason why users return to the drug and find it so difficult to quit: withdrawal feels awful, and addicts use again to feel better, even if they want to quit. It is unlikely that the negative withdrawal feelings play such a causal role in IGD: gamers do not return to the game to alleviate their irritability, but rather because they *want* to play.[7]

Tolerance to drugs causes users to need to use greater doses of their drug of choice to get the same satisfaction or excitement—the same "highs." Tolerance thus helps explain why addicts expose themselves to such negative consequences: users want the high and need increasing quantities to get there, which requires users to engage in behaviors with more potential for negative consequences (stealing, forgoing food, meeting with dangerous dealers, etc.). However, spending increasing time gaming (more "doses") might have nothing to do with chasing a "high," but instead might occur simply because of the types of activities in the game and the player's interests. In MMOs, for example, players will often spend more time playing so they can get specific rare loot drops that will make their character more powerful or they might aspire to beat difficult content which requires repeated tries.[8] Additionally, as one's interest and experience in a hobby deepens, one will seek out more complex and difficult activities in the hobby. A runner might begin with a local 5k and later aspire to run a marathon or a Tough Mudder, but it wouldn't make sense to say that they are clinically addicted to running. For similar reasons, we needn't consider the increase in time spent playing games to be a result of addiction, as it could be a result of one's increase in experience and interest.

Even more puzzling, the APA members who developed the IGD criteria recommend using the "need for powerful [gaming] equipment" to experience the same excitement as before as an additional way of assessing tolerance.[9] Gaming technology evolves rapidly, and one will need to purchase new equipment to play new games, and, unless one desires to be restricted to the kinds of gameplay and graphics that can be held on 4 MB cartridges, they will need to upgrade their ancient SNES eventually. Gamers thus do not game more and get better gaming equipment to chase a high, and so tolerance does not really play the same explanatory role for addictive behavior that it does in substance use disorders.

The inclusion of the withdrawal and tolerance conditions thus make IGD *sound* like an addiction, but it is not clear that these criteria are similar to withdrawal and tolerance in traditional substance addiction, nor is it clear that they are helpful in picking out cases of problematic gaming. However, they might be useful when applied to certain types of games—namely games with a particular kind of structure. Just as the chemical structure of addictive substances contributes to their addictive nature, the way games are structured might facilitate addiction. We discuss this possibility more below, but for now we want to point out that, for many gamers and games, it is likely that the withdrawal and tolerance criteria miss the mark.

The majority of the proposed criteria for IGD therefore do not seem to be indicative of concerning behavior. The remaining three criteria—loss of control, continuing despite problems, and negative consequences—do seem problematic, however. If someone's gaming habit is preventing them from living a fulfilling life, then they would benefit from adjusting their behavior. However, as we argue in the next section, "gaming addiction" might not be the best way of classifying this problem because, unlike drugs and gambling, gaming *can* be an effective means of coping with *problems in living*.

ADDICTION OR PROBLEMS IN LIVING?

Once a disorder is included in the *DSM*, one can be diagnosed with it, and thus receive a treatment plan covered by insurance.

And so, inevitably, as IGD has come closer to being recognized as a disorder, various avenues for gaming addiction treatments have cropped up. You can go to therapists who specialize in video game addiction, enter rehabilitation facilities that promise to break you free of your gaming addiction, or enroll in specialized online self-help programs. One of these online programs, GameQuitters.com, is founded by a self-proclaimed video game addict. If you go to this site, you can take a short quiz to see if you might be an addict (the quiz simply asks a question for each of IGD's diagnostic criteria) and if you say yes to five out of the nine questions (a threshold many gamers are likely to meet, as explained above), you are told that your score is "concerning and should be addressed immediately" and provided with a handy link to the site's guide to quit video games for good. Aside from being told you are an addict in need of immediate help for the low cost of $27, you can also read testimonials from gamers who have gone through the program. The site's founder, Cam Adair, tells his own story of a school career rife with severe bullying, which led him to avoid interacting with his school peers and turn to gaming instead:

> I didn't really enjoy going to school much anymore and hockey wasn't any better. The less I went to school and the less I went to hockey, the more I played video games. They were a place for me to escape to, a place I had more control over my experience . . . For the next year and a half I was depressed, living in my parents' basement, playing video games up to 16 hours a day . . . When I was gaming I didn't have to think about how bad my life had gotten, and how depressed I was.[10]

Although Cam's program encourages problem gamers to quit gaming altogether, it seems clear from his story that the problem wasn't really the games themselves, but rather the hostile social environment he found himself in at school. And, in fact, Cam's story highlights a common reason why people spend a lot of time playing video games: gaming can provide an "escape" from the stresses of life and negative emotional states, as well as provide positive feelings of acceptance, control, and proficiency. Although we don't all face extreme bullying like Cam, we do all face challenges in life: we must deal with set-backs, loss, isolation, and any number of other things that make day-to-day living difficult to manage and cope with. Such challenges constitute, to borrow a phrase from famous maverick psychologist Thomas Szasz, *problems in living*.[11]

Cam used gaming to help him deal with his problems in liv-ing, and this bears resemblance to objects of addiction: the use of drugs to "self-medicate" emotional distress and temporarily escape various life stressors has long been recognized as an important contributing factor to the development of substance addiction.[12] However, there is a critical difference between gaming and more traditional objects of addiction: gaming can be an *adaptive* way of coping with problems in living, whereas more traditional objects of addiction are *maladaptive*. If gaming can be a beneficial way of coping with life problems, but this isn't the case for traditional objects of addiction, then there is even less reason to view it within the addiction framework.

Drugs and gambling provide a temporary rush, but they don't help resolve any underlying problem and instead cause additional difficulties.[13] It is true that games allow us to men-tally distance ourselves from our current life problems, which does make gaming resemble the kind of "escape" that substance users seek. However, "escape" in itself is not necessarily a bad thing: having a brief reprieve from life's hardships is impor-tant. Unwinding with some *Animal Crossing* or the "dangerously" addictive *Candy Crush* can recharge you after a long, hard day. Sure, one can use drugs and alcohol to decompress, but the risks are obviously more severe. Indeed, on this front, playing video games to relax seems far closer to hobbies like knitting, weight-training, and Pinterest-browsing than to drugs and gambling.[14]

Beyond providing a relatively low-risk temporary escape, gaming can play a more active role in dealing with and ultimately overcoming our problems in living. Games can provide an environment to build social connections, which can help us overcome negative emotions. Cam mentions this aspect of gaming in his story, but frames it as negative, as he views these game-based connections as less "real." We've already argued that gaming friendships can be genuine friendships, but we now want to add that forming and maintaining social bonds is especially important when someone is going through difficult times, as such times in life can feel extremely isolating. These feelings of isolation are often the reason people seek out coping mechanisms in the first place, so if gaming can help us form friendships in vulnerable times, then it seems gaming could be a *beneficial* coping mechanism. Furthermore, gaming can offer a way to socialize when life's difficult circumstances make it nearly impossible to do so in person: if someone is taking care of a terminally ill family member, or is battling an illness themselves, or is too strapped for cash to pay the price that many in-person activities cost, or lives in the middle of nowhere, the gaming world may offer the only realistic opportunity to develop relationships during the times when they are most needed.

Story-rich games may also include characters who are going through relatable situations and emotions, and may thus provide the player additional perspectives on how to cope, or, at the very least, reassurance that others might feel similar things. Games can also allow us to work through troubling emotions via role-play. For example, SM recalls a forum thread of *World of Warcraft* players recounting stories of how playing *WoW* helped them deal with their grief over losing their beloved pets. These players found comfort in being able to name their in-game pets after their deceased real-life pets and being able to continue their adventures together digitally.

Many players are drawn to games because they afford them feelings of focus, control, proficiency, and accomplishment.[15] Simply put, gamers like games because they are good at them, and it feels good to be good at something. Unfortunately, for some gamers, these feelings have yet to be found in other activities and this can increase the desire to spend time gaming. Consider Roger from *Poor Kids*, a Frontline PBS documentary that follows four children and their families, providing an inner look at child poverty in America. When discussing what it was like to become poor, Roger says:

> I think the thing I miss the most from having all this happen [i.e. becoming poor] is the internet. I mean, people don't realize what they have until it's gone. And, whew, serious *World of Warcraft* withdrawals, man. Cause, say, in *World of Warcraft*, I'm awesome. I'm a level 85 Paladin. Tank and healer. And in real life, I'm a 14-year-old boy with nothing going for him.[16]

The "withdrawal" language and finding self-esteem in a fantasy game feed into the addiction narrative, but to label Roger a gaming addict would be to misunderstand him. To see this, just replace the *WoW* references with sports or music references: Roger dislikes being poor because he can't afford to play baseball or guitar, and this is really upsetting because in baseball or band, people looked up to him, he had fun, he had friends, but outside baseball or band, he has yet to find anything he is particularly talented at. Indeed, not only does being poor bring additional obstacles, but it also makes him feel worth less than his classmates. This substitution makes clear that unless we are simply unduly biased against gaming as a hobby, Roger's gaming clearly enhances his life.

When it seems like you are failing at everything, your in-game successes can give you hope—you can, in fact, be good at things and accomplish the tasks you set out to accomplish. And sometimes this reminder serves as a much-needed boost in confidence that you simply are not getting IRL and so is an effective way to overcome this problem in living. One gamer struggling with severe depression recounts how the game *Nintendogs* was the only thing that could provide her with goals she felt were achievable for her in her current circumstances: "Looking after my puppies in *Nintendogs*: washing them, feeding them, walking them, playing with them gave me a sense of accomplishment . . . I didn't want to leave the house but I did sometimes to 'walk' the dogs." In short, unlike other objects of addiction, gaming can help one cope with the emotional and social problems that motivate one to seek out gaming in the first place.[17]

I AM STILL JUST A RAT IN A CAGE

There are only certain kinds of things that people get addicted to—it is unlikely that "math homework addiction" will ever show up in the DSM. So, in order to understand why people get addicted to certain things, it is important to consider the properties of the addictive thing itself. With drugs, the answer lies the fact that these substances are structurally similar to molecules in the brain, and so drugs are able to directly alter our brain function. With behaviors like gambling and gaming, the answer is less obvious, but there are likely specific characteristics of gambling and video games that compel us to play them. If this is the case, it would thus not be video games as a whole that are addictive, but specific ways some video games are structured that promotes addictive behavior.[18] What specific characteristics might these be? Lever-pushing rats can help provide an answer.

In the mid-1900s, psychologists became mildly obsessed with seeing just what they could make animals do simply by rewarding them with pellets of food (today, psychologists tend to use tastier foods like Cap'n Crunch, no doubt due to the increasing attention paid to animal welfare). Aside from providing us with adorable instances of dogs giving high-fives and pigeons playing soccer, these studies also provide a wealth of information on how to make humans do things. Psychologists found that if you give an animal a reward after they do a particular behavior, they will likely repeat this behavior again (since they will expect a reward). Some of the more well-known of these experiments involve placing a rat in a cage that has a lever in it. Now, rats don't usually push levers, but they might accidentally bump into the lever. When it does, a food pellet is dropped into the box. This of course excites the rat (who doesn't love getting food pellets from the heavens?), so it will repeat the behavior that led to the food pellet dropping. If no more food pellets drop, it will stop trying to push the lever, but if food pellets do drop after lever pushes, it will make lever-pushing its hobby. It turns out that the extent to which the rat is into its new lever-pushing hobby depends on the *rate of reinforcement*: how often the lever push results in a food pellet. It turns out that the condition that leads to the most lever pushing is when the number of lever pushes that leads to a food pellet is somewhat random and unpredictable from the rat's perspective. You may find this result surprising—it seems like the rat would be more inclined to continue the behavior when the reward is guaranteed, but this is not the case. Although we are not "rat whispers," it is evident that something about the unpredictability of the reward "hooks" the rat into repeating this behavior.[19]

This basic principle applies to humans as well, and it is the basis for how casinos and lotteries design their games in order to draw customers in and maximize their profits. Humans will pull the lever of a slot machine over and over in the hopes that the next pull will yield the jackpot, and it is the unpredictable reward delivery that is part of what makes gambling addictive. Why this is the case is still up for debate, but the current consensus seems to be because of the way it engages the brain's reward system (indeed, one of the main reasons gambling is considered an addiction in the DSM-V is because of evidence that it affects the brain in ways similar to drugs). In addition to the reward structure of casino games, the lights and sounds of slot machines promote gambling behavior by creating an exciting atmosphere in which it seems like everyone is winning all the time. Thus, pretty much everything about the way gambling establishments and their machines are structured is done with the goal of getting people to gamble more.[20]

When it comes to video games and addictive play, this same idea holds—there are certain choices video game designers can make that will result in the game being more difficult to walk away from. Some of these addictive designs are obvious: most infamously perhaps are the "pay-to-win" games that employ loot boxes and other systems that very closely resemble gambling. In such games, players can use real money to purchase random rewards, with the low probability of obtaining powerful upgrades. Such "pay-to-win" mechanics are most obvious in free-to-play mobile games, and their profit often depends on the game's "whale" players who spend a lot of money for upgrades. Though these "pay-to-win" mechanics are typically negatively received by more "serious" gamers, many popular console and PC games include loot box features that award various game features that do not necessarily increase a player's in-game power but are desirable for aesthetic reasons. The random allocation of these valuable rewards is essentially a form of gambling (the United Kingdom has even given serious consideration to including loot boxes under their existing gambling regulation laws), and brings with it the same psychological problems that gambling does: players will, for example, spend their entire college fund trying to get rare FIFA player cards.[21]

Game designers also employ the same unpredictable reward structure of gambling in more subtle ways. These game design choices might not look as similar to gambling as loot boxes do, but they operate on the same psychological principles. By making the timing of rewards uncertain and random, designers encourage players to play continuously: players do not know when they will finally get the reward they want (but know that what they are doing can lead to the reward), and so they keep playing. And, by offering limited-time offers—if you don't play every week, or even every day, you will miss out on loot or story—games promote "fear of missing out" (FOMO), which increases gaming frequency, as well as compulsive feelings.[22]

There are clear financial incentives to structure games like this—a playing gamer is a paying gamer, after all. Despite these psychological problems and the consumer backlash, some developers still defend their decisions. In what is the most down-voted Reddit comment of all time, an Electronic Arts *Star Wars Battlefront 2* representative initially defended EA's choice to allow players to unlock characters either through additional payment or playing roughly the equivalent of a full-time work week for a single hero. Players were justifiably upset: despite the representative's claim that, "The intent is to provide players with a sense of pride and accomplishment for unlocking different heroes," mindlessly grinding isn't an achievement but a hassle, and for an already expensive game, it is in poor taste to ask players to shell out additional money—not to mention the general disdain gamers have for pay-to-win mechanics.

Nevertheless, some game developers have taken steps to try to avoid these psychological traps. *WoW*, for example, has made itself into less of a loot-casino by incorporating various "bad-luck" mechanics for loot. Although rewards are still awarded randomly, they are not endlessly unpredictable: there are now direct ways to progress toward desirable loot if you fail to get it randomly. Taking away the endless grind and replacing it with an end goal to progress toward helps make the game less compulsive: gamers can make progress toward something one day, and then walk away knowing that they can continue making progress in the next game session. The prospect of finally getting that uncertain reward that compels to *play just one more match* or *kill just one more boss* loses some of its hold on us.

We see that some games and aspects of games are problematic in how they encourage compulsive playing; however, this is not true of all games or all aspects of gaming. Importantly, this demonstrates a disanalogy between games and other objects of addiction. When it comes to things like nicotine, heroin, and gambling, the addictive properties can't be extracted from the object itself without ruining the object. For example, you can't remove the opiate from heroin and still engage in the behavior of taking heroin, and if you remove the exciting reward structure from gambling, something lame remains. However, when it comes to video games, the addictive or compulsive aspect can be removed without spoiling the game—indeed, in most cases this would likely improve the game. Additionally, as we argued in the previous section, unlike other objects of addiction, video games can enrich our lives. Finally, although games

Image 4.1 *Candy Casino*

that employ obvious gambling mechanics can be addictive for the same reason that gambling is addictive, in such cases, it makes sense to classify this as a gambling addiction, rather than a gaming addiction, as it is the gambling component that is negatively impacting one's life.

THIS IS YOUR BRAIN ON VIDEO GAMES

We grew up in the "War on Drugs" era, when substantial government effort was made to educate the youth about the dangers of drug use. Perhaps the most memorable (and meme-able) commercial from this campaign drew an analogy between your brain on drugs and a fried egg: "this is your brain on drugs" the announcer declares, as the egg sizzles in the pan. Although there isn't a public campaign about the dangers of video games (yet . . .), we often hear similar sentiments about how video games "fry" the brain, furthering the analogy between drugs and video games.

In case you didn't know, "brain frying" is not a scientific concept, but it captures the idea that something is negatively affecting the brain and, in virtue of this, harming our various psychological, cognitive, and emotional abilities. And there is no shortage of brain studies claiming to demonstrate that video games negatively impact the brain and its functions. In fact, evidence about the way that video games affect the brain influenced the decision to include gaming addiction in the DSM: according to the American Psychiatric Association's brief on IGD, "studies suggest that when these individuals are engrossed in Internet games, certain pathways in their brains are triggered in the same direct and intense way that a drug addict's brain is affected by a particular substance." Evidence from such studies find their way to the public via sensationalized news articles that claim things like "your kid's brain on

Minecraft looks like a brain on drugs" (which, by the logic of transitivity, means your kid's brain looks like a fried egg) and that "playing games is as addictive as heroin."[23]

Although the claim that playing video games affects the brain is often presented by the media as if it is an astonishing finding, it really shouldn't be surprising because *everything* we do affects the brain. The information you get from your environment every second of the day must be processed before it can be acted on, and the brain is an information processing system. If you remove your brain, you aren't going to be doing much of anything—there will be nothing to understand the information coming in from the environment, and nothing to form action plans based on that information. So, it isn't surprising that video games affect our brains—because, duh, of course they do.

But what about the more specific claim that video games affect your brain in the same way drugs of abuse do? Well, this is true in a general sense, but also misleading. Drugs of abuse generally cause excessive release of the neurotransmitter dopamine, which activates the brain's reward pathways, and playing video games also results in a release in the neurotransmitter dopamine. But the catch is, everything we find pleasurable does this, and yet no one is calling for bans of the weekly dopamine-releasing bowling league. The comparison between the effects of drugs vs. games on the brain breaks down when we consider that the chemical properties of the substances *themselves* contribute to their addictive nature—heroin, for example, has a similar chemical structure to molecules in the brain, and because of this structure it is able to bind to receptors in the brain and have all its various effects. Video game pixels (and bowling league wins) cannot directly bind to receptors in the brain in the way that drug molecules can, and so it is unlikely that gaming can promote the same level of long-lasting direct change on the brain's circuitry that addictive drugs can. It's *possible* that certain game reward structures do lead to long-term changes in the brain's reward system, similar to those in substance use disorders. But the research would need to get clear on which specific aspects of video games do this—a general blanket statement that video games engage the brain's reward system alone is simply not enough reason to say that video games as a whole are "as addictive as heroin."

However, although it is safe to say that video games do indeed affect the brain, since literally everything you ever see, hear, touch, taste, and smell affects the brain, it would be a mistake to assume these effects are necessarily those of the "frying" variety. Indeed, some scientists have argued that video games can enhance our cognitive abilities (games "hard-boil" our brains? Perhaps the egg analogy breaks down here). Educational games are obvious examples of the potential for video games to improve our intellectual abilities, and their existence has likely helped video games gain broader acceptance amongst strict parents ("But, Mom, I need a PS5 to help me study!"). Video games can help us learn how to do math, teach us about historical events, and simulate science experiments— but it is unlikely we come home from a hard day of work or school eager to fire up the latest expansion of *Moose Math*. As psychologist Celia Hodent puts the issue, "Too often, apps and games labeled as educational are making unsubstantiated or over-exaggerated claims. And for those that seem to reveal true educational value through standardized scientific evaluation, they might not actually be fun and engaging enough to merit the 'game' label."[24] So the relevant question is: can fun games cognitively benefit us?

There is ample evidence of this; indeed, this is somewhat obvious if you have ever watched e-sport players, especially Real-Time Strategy games (RTS), clicking at lightning speeds. Professional StarCraft II players make about ten actions per second: this means they are not only doing ten physical game actions per second (mouse clicks), but also making decisions about what best to do in the context of the game and planning ahead about what their next moves will be, all while keeping track of what their opponent is doing. This requires the player to mentally keep track of multiple different things at once, while having the physical ability to quickly see what is on the screen and coordinate their movements accordingly.

Of course, very few players have the skill to be professional players, but just as playing recreational sports can improve various physical and mental abilities for causal players, recreational gaming can improve various skills as well. In fact, gamers tend to have better selective attention, are able to switch between multiple different tasks better, and can more readily use information about the current environment to inform behavior. In addition, video game players have better visual perception—they are better able to see small details and distinguish between slight differences in shading—and they are better able to remember visual scenes over a short amount of time. Action games, with their fast-paced and chaotic combat, seem to be especially beneficial for our cognitive and perceptual abilities, and puzzle games, like Tetris, benefit spatial abilities. Finally, video games help players learn new skills and strategies which transfer to other fields and domains of life—players, like students of the liberal arts, "learn how to learn." The evidence is clear: playing video games is far from a mindless activity that rots your brain; instead, it is a cognitively robust activity that relies on technique, strategy, visual perception and spatial abilities, and hand–eye coordination. All that said, skepticism should greet anyone who promises that gaming is a panacea of the mind.[25]

PROBLEMATIC GAMING

Let's be clear, there is such a thing as problematic gaming. As discussed in Chapter 2, players can express all sorts of vices through games—one of which is immoderation (i.e., excessive gaming). Excessive gaming can be problematic when gaming leads to the neglect of other important areas of our life, such as family, friends, work, and school. However, in this chapter, we've argued that addiction might not be the best framework for thinking about excessive gaming because: (a) key elements of the diagnostic criteria fit awkwardly with IGD; (b) unlike other objects of addiction, gaming can be therapeutic; (c) only some aspects of gaming encourage compulsive play and these components can be removed from games; and (d) claims about the gaming-brain being like a brain on drugs are misleading. For these reasons, we think the addiction framework misinforms more than informs. Rather than wean a problematic player off video games like they are a helpless victim of a harmful drug, the goal should be to find a way to integrate games into one's life in a healthier way.

Although problematic gaming is a very real thing, it is also the case that perfectly acceptable gaming activities are thought to be problematic because there are stigmas against gaming. Alexander Kriss, a gamer and therapist, talks about treating a seven-year-old boy, Mickey, whose mother thought he was addicted to Minecraft. However, as things turned out, his mother simply didn't understand her son's favorite pastime. Rather than seeing Minecraft as the enemy of her son, Kriss invited Mickey's mother to learn about the game, to see its value, and to talk with Mickey about why he enjoyed it. What she discovered was that *Minecraft* was far from the mind-rotting activity she initially took it to be; *Minecraft*, she found instead, encouraged creativity, constructive criticism, and sociability.[26] Mickey's mother, unfortunately, isn't alone in assuming video games are worthless time-sucks, as we'll discuss in the next chapter.

KEY POINTS

- Although it is well-accepted by psychologists that problematic gaming exists, there is disagreement as to whether Internet Gaming Disorder (IGD) is a legitimate disorder. In the *DSM-V*, IGD is listed as a "condition for further study," meaning that some psychologists believe that there is evidence in support of it being an actual disorder but that this requires additional investigation.

- Two key criteria of addiction, withdrawal and tolerance, do not fit with IGD. Unlike addictive drugs, one doesn't experience a chemical dependency on games, nor does one acquire tolerance for smaller "doses" of gaming. Accordingly, we see an important disanalogy between IGD and other objects of addiction with respect to the diagnostic criteria.

- Video games, unlike other objects of addiction, can help one cope with problems in living. For example, video games can provide a way to relieve stress, meet friends, and to feel a sense of accomplishment—all without serious risk.

- With traditional objects of addiction, there is a clear chemical connection between the object of the addiction and the brain. However, with respect to gaming, this connection is less clear. That said, there are some games and aspects of games, such as loot boxes, that resemble gambling. However, this points to an important disanalogy: you can remove these aspects of video games without ruining the game, but this isn't true of gambling. When you remove the gambling aspect of gambling, the activity ceases to be gambling.

- In popular media, gaming is sometimes said to affect the brain in a similar way to drugs, but this is a misleading statement for three reasons. First, all pleasurable activities release the neurotransmitter dopamine. Second, with drugs, the chemical properties of the substances *themselves* contribute to their addictive nature, but this isn't the case in games. Third, there is sufficient evidence that games are a cognitively beneficial activity.

Gaming your way out of the cave

The intellectual and aesthetic side of gaming

SOCRATES: They say Thales was studying the stars, Theodorus, and gazing aloft, when he fell into a well; and a witty and amusing Thracian servant-girl made fun of him because, she said, he was wild to know about what was up in the sky but failed to see what was in front of him and under his feet. The same joke applies to all who spend their lives in philosophy.

Plato, *Theaetetus* 174a–b

You open the door to the basement of a lovely older couple's home and are immediately struck by darkness. Squinting, you carefully descend the stairs. Reaching the bottom, you turn a corner and notice an amorphous shadow reflected from a rectangle emanating light. With caution, you approach this strange figure. As you get closer, you see the remnants of soda cans and chip bags and are hit by the stench of staleness, cheese dust particles, and BO. Behold the source of the shadow: it is the couple's adult child, hunched over a gaming controller, with eyes glued to a screen, absorbed in a virtual world while what little life they have in the real world passes them by.

A bit dramatic, but this image captures a common concern that people have about being a gamer: that playing video games is not only a waste of time, but that it is the kind of waste of time that is not befitting of a respectable and responsible adult. Instead, video games are seen as the purview of manchildren who have refused to grow out of their

DOI: 10.4324/9781003308638-6

immature hobby and pursue more serious activities.[1] Despite the fact that adult gaming is probably the most accepted it has ever been, places like Reddit and Quora are replete with people asking if it is acceptable to be an adult gamer. And though many frequently answer in the affirmative, the recurring nature of this question suggests that there are still doubts and even shame about gaming. The "manchild" stereotype is a frequently used joking insult amongst gamers themselves—when someone must leave a group, a commonly heard response is, "Why? Mommy finish making your chicken nuggies for you?" and when someone mentions they can't play because they are busy with adult responsibilities or hobbies, they are met with mocking disbelief that they are finally emerging from their parents' basement. The message is clear: gamers need to grow up, and growing up means that we need to stop playing games.

To illustrate the power that this stereotype and the associated worries have over us, consider a scenario in which you are interviewing for a job that is not in the gaming industry and you are asked about what you like to do in your free time. How likely are you to reveal your gaming hobby? We suspect that you would mention pretty much any other pursuit in this situation. Even if gaming is your main recreational activity, you might instead talk about hiking (you go every couple of months) or playing guitar (you've been meaning to practice more). Why is this the case? Well, when you mention you play music, you are likely to be enthusiastically met with responses that encourage your hobby ("You'll have to play something for me sometime."), while non-gamers typically aren't interested in hearing about your latest virtual conquest (the best response one can hope for from a non-gamer is, "I think my kids play that game, too."). With this kind of response, it's unsurprising that gaming isn't the kind of activity you take pride in disclosing: when you reveal your passion for playing the guitar, you do not feel inadequate or ashamed like you might when revealing your passion for video games.

Thus, even if the previous chapters have convinced you that gaming isn't vicious, you still might worry that gaming is a bad way to spend your life because it is a childish waste of time. Let's call this general concern about gaming the "manchild challenge." The following two chapters comprise our response to this challenge. In this chapter, we argue that we can cultivate and express intellectual and aesthetic virtues through gaming. Since these traits are worthy of being

HEAVEN OR HELL?

Image 5.1 Heaven or hell?

pursued, gaming can be a worthwhile activity after all. In the next chapter, we defend playing video games on the grounds that play itself has inherent value.

WHAT MAKES AN ACTIVITY WORTH DOING?

At the heart of the manchild challenge is an assumption about what activities are (and are not) worth doing. For gamers to overcome this challenge and prove the worth of their hobby, we need to get clear on what exactly makes an activity worth doing. Because the manchild challenge stems from the way society perceives gaming, let's begin our approach to the challenge by thinking about what activities society finds valuable. If society largely views gaming as an unworthy pastime for adults, then what things *are* perceived as being worth doing? If we put down our controllers, what should we pick up in their place? What does gaming lack that the hobbies viewed as worthwhile have? To begin to answer these questions, we can use the "job interview test" as a kind of litmus test for which hobbies can be considered socially acceptable for responsible adults to be doing: given that you don't want your prospective employer to think you're a manchild, are there any hobbies you would consider mentioning in a job interview upon being asked how you like to spend your free time?

There is widespread agreement over the set of activities people would be eager to bring up and the set of activities people would prefer hidden in the deep recesses of their personal browser history. Obviously good things to mention include reading literature, hiking, running a side business, and learning how to program. Obviously bad things include reading smutty romance novels, binge-watching Netflix, gambling, and collecting anime figurines. What separates these two sets? Note that the kinds of hobbies that tend to be praised by society are those that are *productive*—engaging in them yields some desirable outcome, like health, money, or practical skill. Conversely, the hobbies that fail the job-interview test do not lead to anything good and, in fact, may lead to bad outcomes (wasted money, etc.). This suggests that society generally thinks activities are worthwhile insofar as they help to bring about valuable things and timewasters insofar as they do not. The ubiquitous praise of adopting hobbies that can moonlight as money-making "side hustles" exemplifies this way of evaluating the way we spend our free time.[2]

Philosophers refer to this type of value society places on worthwhile hobbies as "instrumental value." Say you have two things, X and Y. If X is valuable because it contributes to Y, then X has instrumental value. If it turns out that Y isn't actually valuable or if it isn't necessary, then X will no longer be valuable either. The value of X thus depends on the value of Y, and so X only has value when it is an "instrument" to getting Y. We will have much more to say on determining the value of the activities we do, but for now it is enough to note society tends to evaluate the worth of activities in terms of instrumental value—what (and how much) is being produced by the activity. Therefore, one way for gamers to prove the worth of gaming is to show that gaming *meets* society's standards of instrumental value by bringing about good things. Let's call this the "meeting strategy" for overcoming the manchild challenge. The good news for gamers is that this is fairly easy to do, due to the recent popular "gamification" trend in education, health, and business.[3]

Gamification involves making ordinarily non-game activities more game-like in order to encourage some desirable behavior. The basic idea is that games are fun, and people like playing them, so if we can make the things that people don't typically enjoy doing more game-like, then people are going to be more motivated to do those things. If your parents ever bought you one of the many educational games on the market in the hope that you'd at least learn something while you spend hours at the gaming console instead of the study desk, then you are familiar with gamification. But gamification isn't just for children who don't want to do their homework: adults have increasingly accepted and embraced "games" that help them improve aspects of their lives. The current ubiquity of fitness trackers and health apps is one of the clearest examples of acceptable gaming: by associating health behaviors with "scores" to achieve, adults are motivated to exercise, drink more water, and eat less sugar. These fitness "gamers" can compete against friends and family for who can be the healthiest, and some health insurance companies now encourage the gamification of health behavior by offering rewards for members who "play." Other popular applications of gamification include language learning (NB enjoys sharpening his Latin skills in Duolingo) and business and marketing (SM is a sucker for star-reward challenges in the Starbucks app), but at this point, gamification is applied in almost every aspect of life because of its supposed effectiveness in motivating people to do things.

The widespread social acceptability of gamification suggests that people think games are worth playing when they help produce some outcome society sees as valuable. After all, no one is calling the guy who strives to complete all the health rings on his Apple Watch a manchild, and we think many instances of gamification would pass the job interview test—playing a game that helps you develop a valuable skill is a worthwhile use of one's free time. Can we end the chapter here and declare the manchild objection defeated? Not so fast. We imagine most gamers are not spending their gaming time engrossed in learning how to conjugate Latin verbs, but are instead blowing up hordes of digital zombies. If we reduce the value of gaming to its instrumental value—what it produces—then most gaming will still be worthless, and gamers will still be manchildren since they are spending time doing something that produces no valuable outcomes. If we want to defend the worth of most gaming, we will need to try a different approach.

The job interview test demonstrates that most people with a modicum of social awareness can easily discern that society perceives *productive* activities to be valuable and unproductive ones not, even if we never really think about the difference. We internalize this way of thinking about value: if society typically equates value with instrumentalilty, we are likely to default to this method as well. But how do we know if society values things correctly? Something might pass or fail the job interview test, but if what society deems valuable is mistaken, then such a test would be worthless in determining an activity's actual value. We are used to thinking about value instrumentally, but producing good outcomes isn't the only way something can be valuable. To understand other ways we can evaluate the worth of something, though, we need an assist from another notorious group of manchildren: philosophers.

HISTORY'S MOST FAMOUS MANCHILD

Although gamers might be the stereotypical manchildren of our era, implying that adults are childish because they partake in worthless activities is a timeless way of insulting people. One of the past targets of the manchild criticism is none other than Socrates, history's most famous philosopher. While criticizing Socrates, Callicles tells him:

> [I]t's not shameful to practice philosophy while you're a boy, but when you still do it after you've grown older and become a man, the thing gets to be ridiculous, Socrates! My reaction to men who philosophize is very much like that to men who speak haltingly and play like children . . . it strikes me as ridiculous and unmanly, deserving a flogging.[4]

Things aren't going much better for us philosophers today, either: as a field of study, philosophy is often seen as a kind of pie-in-the-sky make-believe that distracts from practical and serious stuff. In his recent criticism of higher education, Republican Senator Marco Rubio asserted that "we need more welders and less philosophers."[5] Since philosophy doesn't teach useful and productive skills, it isn't worth studying. Craftspeople can build shelters and roads and doctors can save lives, but what do philosophers do other than annoy people and write books no one will ever read (your present reading material being the exception, of course)? One may even argue that philosophy fails to meet the job interview test as well—what philosophy major hasn't faced jokes about their bleak career prospects (Q: "What did the philosophy major say a year after he graduated?" A: "Do you want fries with that?")?

We can see the similarities to the manchild worry about gaming here: it's fine to philosophize and game when you are a child, but once you grow up, you should be doing the things that contribute to society instead. And if you choose to pursue your childish pastimes instead, others often think such a choice merits, at the least, a verbal flogging in the form of insults and jokes. As both philosophers and gamers, things aren't looking too great for us here. However, philosophers are a contrary bunch, so we are in a good position to defend ourselves. Just as with the manchild challenge to gaming, there is an easy response philosophers can give as well: simply show that philosophy *meets* society's standards of productive, instrumental value.

The meeting strategy has, in fact, been readily employed by philosophers throughout time. For example, when Thales—a philosopher infamous for being so deep in thought that he fell into a well—was mocked for his poverty, he put his studying of the sky to use. Thales successfully predicted that there would be a good olive harvest, and when no one made competing bids, he was able to corner the market. Speaking on this, Aristotle says, "In this way, [Thales] proved that philosophers can easily be wealthy if they wish, but this is not what they are interested in."[6] Philosophers today don't point to the rags-to-riches story of Thales, but we often sing a similar tune about the practical benefits of philosophy in order to justify our department's continued existence in the university budget. Take a journey to the hallways of any philosophy department, and you will likely find the walls plastered with posters attempting to lure in tentative students by proclaiming the external benefits of studying philosophy: it helps you get into the best law, medical, and business schools, bolsters your résumé with important general skills that can be applied to many careers, and increases your lifetime earning potential. We tell students that philosophy majors excel on academic standardized tests and that in repeated studies examining the correlation between college majors and salary, philosophers always fare very well. We entice students by assuring them that studying philosophy doesn't spell financial ruin, but instead can teach you the skills you need to achieve professional success and make more money—if you want to be a lawyer or an olive baron, philosophy can help you reach these goals.[7]

Philosophers and gamers alike can thus employ a meeting strategy in order to justify their value to the world: when we are opening up our copies of Plato's *Republic* or booting up our Xboxes, we are not being manchildren, because we are actually spending our time wisely—these activities can in fact help us develop skills that are beneficial to society, and so they have instrumental value. In principle, there is nothing wrong with the meeting strategy: people need food, shelter, and financial security, and a functioning society requires that its citizens have practical skills and value activities that help develop these. However, the meeting strategy leaves the value of the activity in a tenuous position. If activity X is only valuable because it brings about other valuable things, then defenders of X will find themselves constantly needing to defend the value of doing X (a position philosophy departments find themselves in all the time). And if some other activity W can more efficiently and effectively lead to the things that are actually valuable, then so much the worse for activity X—why spend time on X when you can do W instead? Gaming that does not develop valuable skills would be forever relegated to the manchild category if we were to rely on the meeting strategy alone to justify the value of gaming.

Furthermore, there is something shallow about the meeting strategy. This shallowness is particularly evident when it comes to philosophy: for a subject that has historically been argued to be the path to happiness and wisdom, justifying the practice on the grounds of a solid grad school application or a mid-career salary is a bit underwhelming and seems to miss the point of why people were drawn to philosophy in the first place. Similarly, gamers typically don't find gaming valuable because it will lead to financial gain, better physical fitness, or sharper critical thinking skills—gamers game because they enjoy gaming itself, and any additional benefits that gaming leads to are just bonus perks.

Thankfully, we can borrow a strategy from philosophers to overcome the manchild challenge: what we call a "flipping strategy." Rather than highlighting how philosophy (or gaming) is instrumentally valuable, the flipping approach emphasizes the *intrinsic* value of the activity: the focus of the activity's value is thus not on what it can bring about, but instead is flipped to emphasize the value of the activity itself. However, in order to employ this strategy, we must examine Socrates' objection to society's focus on instrumental value.

THE CAVE AND THE GOOD LIFE

As we noted above, society tends to evaluate things instrumentally, and it's hard to move away from thinking about value in this way, especially since we have been taught it by clever advertisers since we were children. In Plato's *Republic*, Socrates provides us with a metaphor for people who focus only on the instrumental value of their activities: they are like prisoners who spend their lives in a cave, chained in such a way that they only ever see the shadows of objects being cast on the back of the cave wall, rather than actual objects.[8] He asks us to consider what these cave-dwellers would think about the world: because they have been raised in the cave, the shadows are all they have ever experienced in their lives, and so they would assume the world consists of shadows and nothing more. These shadows are meaningful to the prisoners, and their experiences of them are deemed valuable, but this is only because the shadows are all they know. In fact, if they were to leave the cave, they would soon realize that it was a mistake to think the shadows were real and valuable, as they would discover actual objects are much more real and valuable than the shadows.

The cave story is meant to serve as an allegory for society's unreflective acceptance of mistaken and trivial values: in this allegory, we see that the people in the cave are consumed with things of false value, just as people in the real world are—the cave-dwellers focus their lives around the shadows, and people IRL focus their lives on things like wealth, luxuries, and reputation, and are consumed with meaningless entertainment that provides simple pleasures. However, because they don't know any better, they fail to see how they are living a pitiful existence, trapped by their own desires and ignorance. Though life in the cave *appears* good and meaningful from the prisoners' perspective, it isn't. As Socrates put it in Plato's *Apology*, "The unexamined life is not worth living," and if we are stuck in the cave, we can't truly examine our lives because we have such a limited frame of reference.[9] Thus, in order to live a good life, we must leave the cave.

Leaving the cave requires that we reflect on what is really valuable. Once we do this, we can easily see that the problem with thinking about value only instrumentally is that it can't ultimately answer the question of what makes something valuable. We can say an activity is valuable because it produces something else that is valuable, but then how do we determine if the thing the activity produces is valuable? If we say it's because that thing produces something valuable, we just push the question back again. At some point, we need to figure out which things are valuable in *themselves*, or *intrinsically*. We may think an activity is worth doing because it produces money, but then we must ask ourselves: why is money valuable? You might say because it is required to obtain the basic necessities in life, like food and shelter. But why are these necessities valuable? You might say, you need them to stay alive, and while that is true, you must then ask yourself: what should you do with your life?

To escape the loop of chasing instrumental value after instrumental value, we need to think about the *ultimate goal*. Despite differences in background, culture, beliefs, etc., it is safe to say that we all aim at a happy and successful life, or *eudaimonia*. As Plato has Socrates say in the *Symposium*, "There's no need to ask further, 'What's the point of wanting happiness?' The answer seems to be ultimate."[10] And what does leading a happy and successful life look like? Well, our ancient philosophy friends thought that it involved being a particular kind of person: a virtuous person. Recall from our earlier discussions, someone can have material success, but be miserable if they have no real friends (e.g., Scrooge) and have insatiable desires, leaving them always unsatisfied (e.g., the Leaky Jar), and someone can have very little material goods, but still have a fulfilling life if they are a good person (e.g., Socrates was poor and the Stoic Epictetus was a former slave). Becoming a virtuous person involves reflecting on what goodness, knowledge, truth, and beauty are, or simply, by practicing philosophy. Through philosophy, we can flip our understanding of reality and leave the dogmatism that is life in the cave.

But the value of philosophy goes further than this: intellectual activities like philosophy are simply good in themselves. Although slogans like "learning is fun" and campaigns like "The More You Know" may seem like empty clichés meant to motivate bored students, it's likely that many of our readers have had the experience of getting swept into a Wikipedia rabbit hole: you start out looking up something you needed to know, but then something in the article piques your interest and you click on that, only to become curious about another topic, and so on. Or perhaps you have found yourself discussing with friends or daydreaming about absurd scenarios like "Who would win in a fight, Link or Mario?" or "How would I survive in a zombie apocalypse?" and thinking through various outcomes and counters to those outcomes. These idle daydreams are not done for any particular reason—they are simply fun to think about. Such phenomena demonstrate a fundamental aspect of human nature: we enjoy intellectual activities for their own sake. As the famous philosopher Aristotle puts it, "All human beings by nature desire to know," an idea echoed by the famous aardvark Arthur in the statement, "Having fun isn't hard when you've got a library card."[11] We are curious and inquisitive creatures who are imbued with a deep-seated motivation to know. One does not need to be an academic philosopher to appreciate the intrinsic value of intellectual activity—everyone from the child asking their parent why the sky is blue, to the amateur naturalist cataloging plant species observed on a hike, to the football fan thinking about various counterfactual scenarios from last night's game is demonstrating a love of learning. Activities that involve understanding and reflecting are deeply satisfying to us and do not require any external outcomes to make them valuable—learning may lead to valuable social outcomes, like money, grades, and status, but it is also good in itself, as is clearly shown by the fact that we pursue such activities in absence of any material benefit.

Intellectual activities, as contemporary philosopher Zena Hitz puts it, "cultivate the inner life."[12] Contemplation involves learning about something and appreciating it for its own sake—going beyond appearances and seeking a deep understanding of what is valuable about it. It is through contemplation that we discover what is meaningful about an activity, which in turn enables us to deliberately choose meaningful pursuits.

In response to the manchild challenge, philosophers argue that philosophy only seems worthless because most people are stuck in the cave, concerned with superficial things. The allegory of the cave helps us see how we can flip our understanding of value: philosophy may not appear to be valuable when we look at it through the lens of what society generally finds valuable, but once we realize that society's understanding of value can be mistaken, we see that intellectual activities like philosophy are not only a means of apprehending what is valuable, but also valuable activities in themselves.

ARE GAMERS CAVE-DWELLERS?

Plato deals critical damage to Callicles' criticism of philosophy with the flipping strategy, but can gaming use a similar strategy to overcome the manchild challenge? Though gaming shares many of the same criticisms of philosophy and can utilize a similar meeting strategy, it isn't clear that the flipping strategy will work for gaming. For starters, think about the fundamental aims of philosophy vs. gaming: leaving aside the oddballs on either side, people do not crack open a philosophy book to be entertained and they do not boot up their gaming consoles to achieve enlightenment. Even if philosophy seldom achieves it, it at least aims at wisdom, while video games seem most obviously to aim at entertainment, not knowledge. Many of the greatest minds in history have been philosophers, while it is far from clear that the same can be said for gamers, despite what the average gaming forum poster tells you.

The most glaring hurdle to gaming's use of the flipping strategy, though, is that gaming seems to be a quintessential example of an activity that would occur in the allegorical cave: gaming, after all, involves engaging with a simulated reality. Socrates describes those who are stuck in the cave as "lovers of sights and sounds," which seems a fitting description of gamers as they stare at their flashing screens with the sounds of explosions and gunfire blaring in the background.[13] Our stereotypical manchild gamer even resides in a cave-like environment—the basement of his parents' house! One might argue that gaming serves as a paradigmatic case of an activity that encourages distraction from meaningful contemplation—when we turn on our consoles, we turn off our minds.

Indeed, Hitz has offered such a view of gaming. In her MC Hammer-endorsed book *Lost in Thought*, Hitz agrees that engaging in contemplative activities is integral to living a good life, and she defends the idea that even mundane interests and pursuits that occupy the minds of normal humans in everyday life can serve as "objects of contemplation."[14] Activities that encourage contemplation are the ones that prod us to dig deeper, to appreciate not only their goodness, but also why they are good. Many ordinary things can do this: nature, family, math, carpentry, and reciting Psalms are all included in her list of potential objects of contemplation. Notably absent in her list of contemplative activities is playing video games because, on her view, it is not the type of activity that encourages reflection—instead, it provides us with trivial experiences that distract us from meaningful thought. In contemplative activities, she states, "[T]he intellect reaches past whatever is given in immediate experience. That is why mere experiences sought for their own sake (video games, channel surfing, pornography) do not count." Furthermore, even if someone takes up video games in a contemplative spirit, Hitz believes they will soon find themselves "drawn into the compulsive pursuit of distraction, to cascading, increasingly joyless victories in pixels."[15]

So, in Hitz's view, certain activities, by the nature of their subject matter, have greater power to encourage contemplation than other activities, even if one does not begin the activity with contemplation in mind. Math is such an activity: students might initially pursue math for external reasons (course credit, impressing others, etc.), but come to appreciate the subject for intrinsic reasons (e.g., they marvel at its rational structure.). Video games, on the other hand, join the noble company of pornography, heroin, and binge drinking in having the reverse power. Rather than inspiring us to intellectual heights, they tether us to pointless, simple pleasures that distract from reality. One doesn't discover one's true self through watching inane cat videos on YouTube or through a bender, but through activities like art, music, sport, teaching, and helping others. If Hitz is right, gamers really would be like the cave-dwellers—absorbed with the shadow puppet shows, distracted from seeking a deep understanding of the world.[16]

CONTEMPLATION, FICTION, AND INTERACTIVITY

It's undoubtedly the case that many games are simple and mindless, and though enjoyable, are played merely as a way to distract oneself from reality for a bit (sometimes they even serve as distractions from distractions, as the many of us who piddle away at phone games while watching TV can attest). However, there are many games that do provoke thought, from quality indie games such as *McDonald's Video Game*, which encourages the player to reflect on various corporate business practices, to mainstream games such as the *BioShock* series, which has players reflect on the philosophy of Ayn Rand, among many other things. Insofar as games serve as objects of contemplation, playing them is an intrinsically valuable activity.

In this section, we will argue that the narrative structure and the player's role in the game can make games an especially effective means of provoking thought.

Take, for example, a scenario from the popular and critically acclaimed game Mass Effect 3. Players must choose whether to cure a disease that was intentionally given to a race of aggressive aliens, the Krogan, in order to prevent them from breeding too much, or to keep the disease in place and ensure that the Krogan population stays low and their tendency for violence will not cause another galactic war. This choice is situated within a morally complex background story. On the one hand, the player must reflect on the state of the Krogan— how the Krogan species has been wronged and deceived in the past and how they are currently facing despair, hopelessness, and in-fighting due to their inability to successfully have families. But on the other hand, they must consider the potential destruction and death the Krogan may cause—that is, the behaviors that caused other species to deploy the virus against them in the first place.

Mass Effect 3 thus presents us with a kind of interactive thought experiment.[17] Thought experiments have been used by philosophers for millennia as a way of provoking contemplation on difficult or abstract topics by providing more concrete hypothetical situations we can work through in our imagination. The famous "trolley problem" is an example of a thought experiment, and it bears a striking resemblance to Mass Effect's genophage cure scenario in what it asks us to contemplate. The trolley problem presents us with a dilemma: a train is headed down the tracks toward several people, and we have the option to pull a lever, causing the train to switch tracks and head toward one poor sap. Generally, it seems worse if more people die than fewer, but it also seems worse to kill someone rather than to merely let them die. What is puzzling about the trolley problem is that in order to prevent more people from dying, it seems that we must kill a person. So, we must choose between an act that kills one person or an omission that kills several. Would you pull the lever?

This is an interesting and worthwhile question, but notice, we know no details about anyone in the scenario. In fact, when thought experiments like this are brought up in class, students often ask about the details—do any of the people have kids? Is the one person a doctor or a criminal?, etc. Philosophy teachers usually respond by telling students that, like any experiment, we must hold different variables constant, and thus must assume that all the background information is the same. But, of course, nothing in life is like that—life is messy.

This is where the interactive-thought experiments found in video games have an advantage over traditional thought experiments: unlike traditional philosophical thought experiments, which often provide a very bare-bones description of the situation we are supposed to imagine, video games offer thick descriptions about the world and the characters in it. *Mass Effect* 3 puts us in a similar situation to the trolley problem in which we face a moral conflict and must make a difficult choice. However, unlike the trolley problem, which keeps us at the level of the abstract and general, *Mass Effect* 3 operates at the level of the particular.[18] We are immersed in the gritty details of the politics of the Citadel and their ramifications, forced to make a choice, and the immersive and interactive nature of the game puts our agency front and center in ways that philosophy's thought experiments cannot.

Furthermore—and returning to a point from Chapter 1— the imaginary/fictitious nature of interactive thought experiments provides a mitigating context for violent or immoral conduct that occurs in-game, allowing us to explore various consequences of our actions in low-stakes conditions. It would be terrible if a trolley situation occurred in real life (or if you had to be the one to pull the lever). But because the morally complex scenarios in video games occur in a fictional world, they provide occasion to stop and reflect upon the ethically relevant dimensions of the situation when we make our decision. Marcus Schulzke calls these opportunities "moral exploration": instead of teaching a clear moral lesson to players, the interactive nature of video games allows players to explore different choices and, given the fictional nature of the game, no one is harmed by making a "bad" choice.[19]

The moral exploration that occurs in games isn't purely intellectual, though. Like in the mediums of theater, film, and books, moral contemplation about video game narratives occurs in conjunction with emotion. Indeed, the emotional response plays a pivotal role in moral and aesthetic reflection, according to Martha Nussbaum. Speaking about tragic poetry, she writes:

> Our cognitive activity, as we explore the ethical conception embodied in the text, centrally involves emotional response. We discover what we think about these events partly by noticing how we feel; our investigation of our emotional geography is a major part of our search for self-knowledge.[20]

However, although all works of fiction provide situations that can provoke contemplation on morally difficult situations, the interactive nature of video games distinguishes them from these other mediums like books and movies. For example, in *Avengers: Infinity War*, we watch Scarlet Witch make the choice to kill the person she loves, Vision, in order to prevent Thanos from getting the Mind Stone and killing half of the population, and we understand how difficult this choice must be. We can reflect on what things she must be thinking and feeling, but simply watching another character face a moral dilemma is different from playing as the character who must make the choice, and then play out the consequences. As Grant Tavinor explains, in "traditional narrative fiction, the appreciator is a passive and distanced subject having no effect on the fictional world" and thus the emotions experienced are primarily *relational*: we sympathize or empathize with the characters and situations. But with video games, "the emotions are in the majority *self-directed* ones, and the emotionally propelled learning is often about the player's own role in the fictional world."[21] Jon Robson and Aaron Meskin describe something similar when they argue that video game fictions are "self-involving interactive fictions." Gamers become a part of the fiction, and thus "the player's actions genuinely make things *about the player* true in the fiction of the video game." Just as children are the characters they play in make-believe, players are "characters in the fictional worlds associated with video games."[22] Other modes of fiction can provide detailed descriptions, but they are unable to place the thinker in the role of the one actually making the choice, like video games can. As such, gamers experience a unique and vibrant intellectual and emotional experience.

Now it might be the case that the literary quality of games hasn't reached the level of, say, Proust and Milton—perhaps it never will—and many themes in video games are well-traversed in science fiction and fantasy.[23] However, objects of contemplation needn't be restricted to the artifacts of stuffy museums or your literature professor's personal library; popular science fiction, fantasy, and mystery novels are certainly capable of inspiring reflection. Furthermore, games are not novels, and for narrative-based games, it makes sense to assess the combination of gameplay and story, rather than the story alone—video games are *games*, after all.[24] Consider *Detroit: Become Human*. The game is set in Detroit in the year 2036. Human life has been revolutionized by the development of androids, AI beings who resemble humans. Many jobs that humans once did are now done by androids: caretakers, janitors, nannies, military and police officers, teachers, and professional athletes are now androids. Humans largely treat androids as objects, and with unemployment and poverty on the rise, animosity towards androids has increased. The conflict intensifies as androids become deviants (that is, capable of making independent choices based on their own thoughts and desires) and no longer simply do what they are ordered. The game explores the trope of whether AI beings should have political and moral rights, and it does it against the background of real historical racial inequality.

What separates *Detroit* from media that explores similar themes, like the film *Her* and Philip K. Dick's *Do Androids Dream of Electric Sheep?*, is how the gameplay interacts with the story. Like the *Mass Effect* series, the game employs a branching mechanic in which the choices you make alter the story. The narrative is told through a mix of NPC discussion, background settings, reading material you discover, and cutscenes. The story places the player in the perspective of three different characters: Connor, an Android police officer in charge of policing deviant Androids; Markus, an Android caretaker who initiates an Android revolution; and Kara, an Android housekeeper who develops maternal affection for a young girl, Alice. As the game develops, the three stories converge in an intense way.

Connor, for instance, is trying to track down both Markus and Kara for crimes they have committed, thereby placing the player in a unique perspective. When we decide how Conner should act toward Kara and Marcus, several considerations arise: the narrative drives us to consider Conner's own goals and social pressures as a cop while also worrying about Kara and Markus, since the player is intimately aware of their circumstances, having occupied their points of view as well. The player thus makes decisions while occupying and balancing various perspectives at once, bringing depth to narrative elements that might be considered tropes.

THE AESTHETICS OF GAMEPLAY

In the previous section, we saw that story and gameplay can play a central role in provoking reflection and imagination in gaming, activities which are good in themselves. However, not all games have narratives, and thus we might wonder what aesthetic and intellectual value games can have apart from their narrative content. That is, what aesthetic and intellectual value does gameplay itself have?

Before we answer this, let's take a step back and think about why we can ask the question about what is worth doing in the first place. The whole idea that we can judge the worth of how ourselves and others spend their time is premised on our ability to *choose* how we spend our time. It makes sense to ask whether it is a more worthwhile use of a person's weekend to snooze the day away or go out birdwatching, but there is something nonsensical about asking the same question about how your dog spends her time. Your dog cannot meaningfully understand and evaluate various options, and then choose how to spend her time based on this reflection, but you can.

Why It's OK to Be a Gamer

This is one of the greatest strengths (and heaviest burdens) of possessing a human mind: along with our ability to engage in rational thought comes the power to weigh and evaluate reasons and choose our course of action based upon this reflection—our ability to be *agents*.

When we game, we are also agents. In fact, the player's way of being an agent is arguably the fundamental aspect of games. Think about the basic design of most games: there is some goal a player is given, and some set of abilities that the player is given to reach that goal. The player must then decide how to use these abilities within the parameters of the game in order to achieve the goal. Even in sandbox games, which lack clear objectives, players are agents, using the tools and rules the game gives them to accomplish the goals they set for themselves. As the philosopher C. Thi Nguyen explains:

> The game designer crafts for players a very particular form of struggle, and does so by crafting both a temporary practical agency for us to inhabit and a practical environment for us to struggle against. In other words, the medium of the game designer is agency. If you want a slogan, try this one: games are the art of agency.[25]

When we play different games, we thus experience different "agential modes"—different ways of being an agent, determined by the abilities and constraints given to us by the game design. For example, for most of the zombie apocalypse RPG *Last of Us*, you play as the character Joel, a grizzled badass who has spent the last 20 years doing whatever it takes to survive the fall of society. When you play as Joel, you have the ability to expertly wield all kinds of guns, melee weapons, and bombs, but your ammo and material for crafting is severely limited. As the player, then, you have the ability to go out guns blazin' and light up the nearby enemies, but you have to decide if this is a good use of your limited resources, given that there are probably more zombies a few rooms down. The game design thus gives the player the abilities of a strong warrior with the constraint of careful resource management, greatly adding to the "surviving the apocalypse" feel of the game. The agential mode involves thinking carefully about how you will navigate enemies given your limited resources. Later in the game, players are exposed to a different agential mode when they play as Ellie, a 14-year-old girl. During a critical fight, Ellie has escaped imprisonment with only a small knife, and she must fight off a gun and machete-wielding leader of cannibals. Instead of facing the enemy head-on, as you could when playing as Joel, you must now rely on stealth. Though the game mechanics and overall goals are the same between both characters, the game feels very different because of the expansion of abilities in one, and the diminution in the other. And this is just a switch of agential modes in one game—think about all the different ways you can play the many different types of games. Each game provides the player with a different set of abilities and constraints, and thus a different agential mode.

Once we begin to look at how the goals, rules, mechanics, and setting affect the gameplay, we can come to appreciate the aesthetic and intellectual experience found in games that lack narrative richness. *Mario Kart* and *Among Us* don't have much in the way of storylines, but each provides a unique orientation toward the game. In *Among Us*, players must try to detect who the imposter is while they complete tasks, while the imposter must try to kill players without others knowing they are the killer. The game requires the combination of Sherlock Holmes' "deduction" and the manipulation of Loki. In contrast, although *Mario Kart* isn't a mindless activity, it relies more on reflexes, dexterity, and often a little luck of the shell.

So, just as playing games with different narrative and fictional elements can expose us to a variety of ideas and feelings, playing games with different gaming elements exposes us to different ways of doing things. This is an *intellectually* valuable experience, as it expands our "library" of agential modes.[26] Navigating successfully through life requires us to play different roles, each with slightly different demands—the same person may be a child, parent, friend, teacher, student, employee, and supervisor all at the same time. Each of these roles has different goals and requires different abilities and skills to do well. As agents, we can choose how we approach each of these roles, and these choices determine how well we perform. When we are considering how to be a good teacher, we must consider what the goals of teaching are and then think about how we can deploy our skills and what we must do to achieve this goal. When we are considering how to be a good friend, the goal will be slightly different from the goal of teaching, and thus we must think about how to deploy our skills in a different way. The more exposure we have to different ways of being an agent, the better agents we can be in any role we take up.

Additionally, gaming provides valuable *aesthetic* experiences of agency. Games are designed so that the goals are achievable, but their achievement is challenging. This provides a particular type of aesthetic experience of *struggle*, in which the player feels a harmony between their abilities and the challenges of the gameplay world.[27] Players must push their skills to the maximum to cope with the situation, resulting in a feeling of fit between themselves and the world. MMO raiding is a great example of this experience: on the most difficult fights, you must react to what the boss does and maintain your ability rotation, all while coordinating your movement with the rest of the players on your raid team. Successfully doing this can take hundreds of attempts, but when you finally get it right, everything "clicks" and there is a feeling of flow between you, the fight, and the other players.

Gamers can gracefully or noobishly deploy their skills to overcome in-game obstacles, and there is beauty in skilled performance.[28] And just as an athlete can develop new techniques, plays, and strategies, so too can gamers—hence, gaming allows us to express and cultivate creativity. In PvP games this might take the form of baiting an opposing player into an unfavorable situation by having hidden teammates, concealed abilities, or by planting a trap. In PvE games, this can involve devising new strategies for defeating a boss or solving a puzzle. In buildcrafting games, players are given immense freedom for how they can confront the challenges in the game. For instance, in *Destiny 2*, players can choose which class they want to play as (Hunter, Warlock, or Titan), and within each class are various subclasses (Arc, Void, Solar, Stasis, and Strand), and within each subclass are various abilities the player can choose from (too many to list). The player, then, can think about how to effectively combine their abilities with weapons and armor—each comes with their own unique qualities. Accordingly, there are many ways to play any single encounter; players are given a great deal of freedom and flexibility for how they want to play. Finally, there are straightforwardly creative genres of games. Sandbox games like the immensely popular *Minecraft* allow players to be creative by designing and building worlds. *Minecraft* players have designed escape rooms, recreated the entire *Game of Thrones* continent, and developed their own video games within *Minecraft*.[29]

GAMING OUT OF THE CAVE

Even if we can overcome the worries about immoralism and addiction discussed in the previous chapters, we may still encounter the problem that gaming is perceived by society to be a waste of time, better replaced by more worthwhile activities. We have argued that this "manchild challenge" to gaming depends on a conception of value that focuses on productivity, and in order to overcome this challenge, we modeled our defense of gaming off the responses philosophers have given to a similar challenge to the value of philosophy. Society's evaluation of activities depends on a superficial notion of value, like the false images the cave-dwellers perceive in Plato's allegory of the cave. In order to leave the cave, we must flip our understanding of value by reflecting on what activities are constitutive of a happy and meaningful life— these are the activities that are valuable in themselves, independently of what they produce.

We have argued that gaming can be such an activity. Narrative-rich games can provoke contemplation, and their interactive nature can deepen our reflection. As such, games can help us expand our imagination and emotional repertoire and gain a deeper understanding of the world. Apart from the narrative elements, games also allow us to explore different modes of agency and express skill, grace, and creativity. If intellectuals are willing to argue that it is a misunderstanding of value to see art, literature, music, and philosophy as childish or trivial, then they should be willing to admit that it is a misunderstanding of value to say the same of games also, as games, too, have intellectual and aesthetic value.

KEY POINTS

- The "manchild challenge" asserts that gaming is an immature hobby. For example, gaming doesn't pass the "job interview test," which assesses value in terms of productivity. By drawing a parallel with philosophy, we meet the manchild challenge.

- Philosophers, both past and present, face the manchild challenge, too. They adopt two strategies for responding to this challenge: the "meeting strategy" involves showing that philosophy can pass the job interview test, and the "flipping strategy" involves showing that the job interview test is superficial. Through philosophy, one can discover what really matters and engage in an intrinsically valuable activity.

- The gamification movement is really just an iteration of the meeting strategy. It aims to vindicate the value of gaming by demonstrating how it increases productivity. The problem is that these games are not typically the games of gamers, and these motives hardly seem to capture what drives the passion of gamers.

- However, gaming can adopt the flipping strategy, too. The interactive narratives of gaming can provoke ethical reflection and deepen our imagination, and gaming, in general, can develop our agency and creativity and allow us to express skill and grace.

Both work and leisure are necessary, but leisure is better than work and is its end; and therefore, the question must be asked, what ought we to do when at leisure? Clearly, we ought not to be playing, for then play would be the end of life . . . [But] play is needed more amid serious occupations than at other times (for he who is hard at work has need of relaxation, and play gives relaxation, whereas work is always accompanied by exertion).

Aristotle, *Politics* 8.3.1337b33–41

So far, we have spent the chapters of this book arguing that playing video games can contribute to cultivating a virtuous character. Through gaming, one can develop virtues like fortitude and moderation (Chapter 2), build deep, meaningful friendships (Chapter 3), release stress and improve cognitive abilities (Chapter 4), and experience and reflect on brilliant aesthetic properties (Chapter 5). Character, friendship, intelligence, and reflection are central to living well, and thus, in so far as gaming develops these traits, gaming is part of the good life. You might think we can stop with the philosophy and return to video games now, resting assured that gaming's value has been secured.

And perhaps we should end here, as we are about to challenge some of what we have done throughout the book. But what fun would that be? And what fun would gaming be if it were all about cultivating virtue and not about play? This

DOI: 10.4324/9781003308638-7

is actually an important question—if you've been following along so far in this book, you may have noted that we have missed a glaringly obvious response to the question of why it is OK to be a gamer: that gaming is an *enjoyable* activity. In fact, when SM first mentioned to one of her gaming friends that she was writing a book on what makes gaming a good activity, his response was, "Isn't it just because gaming is fun?"

There are a couple reasons why we have avoided the obvious answer up until now. First, a book pitched with the thesis "gaming is fun" is not likely to land a contract. More seriously, fun-ness is not necessarily connected with goodness—just imagine a serial killer justifying their hobby by appealing to how enjoyable it is to kill people. But now that we have unpacked what the good life is and what things contribute to it, it's time to seriously consider the role that unserious activities, divorced from their contributions to noble things like kindness, friendship, and creativity, can play in the good life.

It's important to consider this because the primary motivation for gaming isn't its role in cultivating virtue. Instead, for the most part, gamers are drawn to games because they are fun and engaging. Moreover, there is something pernicious about needing to appeal to an activity's usefulness to justify doing it. As Aristotle puts it, "To be asking all the time what use something is, is highly inappropriate for people who are great-souled and free."[1] Although games can provide all sorts of benefits, from helping us make friends to provoking contemplation, it is the thrill, freedom, and pure enjoyment that drives us to play. Indeed, if one justifies play only by appealing to some further good that play brings about, one overlooks the virtue of play itself and misses out on a main component of the life well-lived. To see this point, it's time to leave the company of our ancient philosophy pals and instead join forces with grasshoppers.

ALL PLAY AND NO WORK MAKES
YOU DIE IN THE WINTER

Let's start out with a familiar enough dichotomy: work and play. In daily life, work and play are commonly defined as being antithetical to each other, and their diametric opposition is poignantly captured by the philosophical minds of 80s rock bands: "Everybody's working for the weekend," asserts Loverboy, and The Bangles express a desire shared across humanity when they proclaim, "I wish it was Sunday, 'Cause that's my fun day, My I don't have to run day." Working is something we do because we *need* to do it to get something else—we don't choose work for itself. The weekend break from work is what makes working worth it, as it is during the weekend when we freely decide how we want to spend our time. Weekend time is fun—it is playtime. Play, as opposed to work, is not done for anything at all, and this is precisely why it is enjoyable. When we spend our time playing, we are free from all other concerns except the enjoyment of the activity. We are not aiming to make money, or to gain knowledge, or to improve ourselves in any way. We are instead just relishing the time we have, freely pursuing whatever it is we like to do, simply because we like to do it.

But one might argue that the aimlessness of play makes it a superfluous, unnecessary addition to an adult's life. Play is the domain of children, and for good reason, one might think: since play does not lead to anything, it also cannot contribute anything of value in our lives. In fact, one might argue that time spent in play is wasted for this very reason. Play might be fun, but why spend time playing when you could be doing something more useful? And if you do spend time playing, you better make sure you leave aside enough time for work, since all the important stuff in life requires work.

The danger of an all-play-no-work lifestyle has been immortalized in Aesop's fable "The Grasshopper and the Ants." In the tale, a hungry grasshopper begs a group of hard-working ants for food so he can survive the winter. The ants are surprised by his request—surely, the grasshopper stored food for the winter? The grasshopper explains that he was so busy singing in the summer that he didn't have time to work. The ants admonish him: "If you spend the summer singing, you can't do better than spend the winter dancing."[2] As with all fables, "The Grasshopper and the Ants" is not just a story, but serves as a way of teaching children an important life lesson: in order to survive, you can't just play around all the time—you have to do things you don't want to do. It sucks, but them's the breaks, kid.

The importance of work is reiterated as we grow up, and the ants among us sacrifice doing what we want to do—whether it be going out and partying, mindlessly scrolling social media, or playing video games—to get good grades, climb the corporate ladder, and make money. And as we are busy working, we sadly bear witness to what happens to our grasshopper acquaintances: they fail out of school, wind up at dead-end jobs, and generally live messy unstable lives. Aesop seems like he hit the nail on the head with this particular fable: although fun in the moment, the grasshopper's all-play-no-work life doesn't pan out in the long-run, and isn't a life we should choose. In order to survive and thrive, we must spend at least some of our time working. In fact, you might even believe that the value of play as an adult is that it facilitates better work. Such is the attitude espoused by tech companies that build fun office spaces with "work hard, play hard" cultures. On such a view, play is not good in itself, but good because it makes us more productive.

We dedicated the previous chapter to explaining the problems with equating value solely with productivity, so you should already be skeptical that a purely productivity-oriented life (in keeping with the fable, an *ant-approach* to life) would be a good life. We argued that, instead, the truly valuable activities are those that contribute to the ultimate goal of *eudaimonia*—the good life. But, as our friends Aristotle and Plato have taught us, the virtuous life is a project, and cultivating good character is an ongoing process—it is something we are always *working* toward. The operative word here is *work*, the antithesis of play. *Eudaimonia* and cultivating good character are, of course, their own rewards—they are intrinsic goods, after all—but the good life ain't always the easy life, which is why it requires work. In fact, we might feel drawn back into the allegorical cave because it's simply *easier* to surround ourselves with distractions and trivial pleasures. To a certain extent, our ancient philosophy friends might thus agree with the tech bros (but for different reasons) that an ant-like attitude is required for a good life—we should live as Virtue Ants, perhaps.[3]

However, we can push back against the idea that work is an essential part of the good life by imagining a perfect society in which all of the citizens' needs are met, all of their desires are instantaneously fulfilled, and all of their interpersonal conflicts have been solved. Everyone is fed and housed and healthy, and there is no more oppression or violence or any other kind of social or environmental injustice—people are living in what is classically referred to as *Utopia*. In such a Utopian society, working would no longer be *required*, since there would be nothing to work for. Without a need to prepare for the allegorical winter, we would be free to do whatever activities we want to do for their own sake. What should we do under such conditions? Which activities would be constitutive of a good life? Should we continue working, or should we, perhaps, play?

WHEN IN UTOPIA, DO AS GRASSHOPPER DOES

In Bernard Suits' book *The Grasshopper: Games, Life, and Utopia*, Grasshopper poses this very question. In this book, we get Grasshopper's side of the story as he willingly accepts the lethal consequences of spending the summer at play. Following the path of Socrates and Jesus, Grasshopper will die for his cause—not philosophy nor the sins of humanity, but something even nobler: playing games. It is because of his commitment to the value of play that Grasshopper refuses to work, even though this refusal is killing him. And though Grasshopper is aware that his death will be treated as an austere lesson by ants, he argues that *he* should be "the hero of the tale," since "if there were not winters to guard against. . .the life of Grasshopper would be vindicated and that of the ant absurd."[4]

The Grasshopper's defense of play hinges on his argument that gameplaying is the only activity that would make sense to choose in Utopia, and because of this, it is the most valuable activity we could be doing. In Utopia, there is no point in pursuing productive labor since our needs and desires are satisfied. For similar reasons, any activity which has its value found in overcoming some deficiency would not be a Utopian activity. The surprising result of this line of reasoning is that many of the activities that we argued are valuable in Chapter 5 would actually be pointless in Utopia, according to Grasshopper. There would be no need, for example, for political and moral activities since everyone has whatever goods they want and is already morally sound. Intellectual inquiry is also not a Utopian activity: since no one is deficient in knowledge, there is nothing to learn. Even artistic pursuits would lose their value in Utopia: art is either connected to passions absent in Utopia (e.g., sorrow, grief, frustration) or is purely formal (e.g., abstract art), in which case computers can produce it.

The situation in Utopia is not that dissimilar to the situation of children during summer break: without the *need* to do anything, there seems to be nothing to do! And just as kids might find themselves complaining about boredom when they find themselves without responsibilities to attend to, we might worry that life in Utopia is too boring to be good. Activities (or at least good, non-boring activities) seem to need some kind of desirable end to make them worth doing (nobody finds staring at the wall a good activity after all), and with all the desirable ends in Utopia met, it seems like there might be nothing worthwhile to do.

But Grasshopper argues there is one worthwhile activity to do in Utopia: playing games (uncoincidentally, the same type of activity many children take up to alleviate their boredom). When everything has already been achieved, we need an activity "in which what is instrumental is inseparably combined with what is intrinsically valuable, and where the activity is not itself an instrument for some further end"; that is, an activity we are not doing because we want to achieve something else, but rather because we want to do the activity itself. "Games meet this requirement perfectly," argues Grasshopper, since games invent goals and obstacles just so that we can do the activity (playing the game).[5]

In other words, gameplaying is the essential Utopian activity because its value is essentially contained in itself. Obstacles in games are created for the purpose of playing the game, not for some further reason. For example, the traffic in Frogger isn't there as part of research into the habits of amphibians facing residential and commercial development, and hurdles are not placed on a track because this makes traveling more efficient. Instead, traffic and hurdles are included because they make frogging and hurdling possible. Accordingly, the activity of frogging and hurdling is taken up for the sake of frogging and hurdling itself, whereas, argues Grasshopper, even things like inquiry are taken up for the sake of something else, like gaining knowledge. Therefore, gameplaying is the genuine Utopian activity, the activity that is the "ideal of existence" because the goals in games are taken up so that we can play the game. The great thing about gaming is that we don't need to look outside of the game itself to find its value, and this is precisely why Grasshopper is willing to die for it: if the value of all other activities depends in part on the outcome of the activity, then they cannot be as valuable as gaming, which needs no other justification. In refusing to work, Grasshopper is standing by his claim that gameplaying is the ultimate valuable activity. You may think yourself a true gamer, but you've got nothing on Grasshopper.

UTOPIAN GAMEPLAYING WOES AND WHIMSIES

Grasshopper's argument is quite novel: it isn't often that philosophers defend gameplaying as the supreme human activity (classically, philosophy has played that role).[6] There is also a certain whimsical appeal to the idea that the life of gaming is the ideal life. There are, however, some problems with Grasshopper's argument. The argument proceeds via the process of elimination: once all other promising candidates for being the key Utopian activity are eliminated, gameplaying is left the victor. However, there is reason to think that some of the activities that Grasshopper excludes from Utopia could very well be Utopian activities. For example, although Grasshopper eliminates morality and art because they are rooted in defects that would not exist in Utopia, not all moral and artistic activity require defect. Art can express wonderful things like joy, friendship, and the feeling found in looking at puppies— none of which are rooted in human imperfection. And there is a much broader dimension of ethics than correcting moral problems. For example, developing creative and novel ways to act ethically could be a Utopian activity.[7] Grasshopper also dismisses inquiry as a Utopian activity because it is rooted in discovering answers, and in Utopia, there is nothing more to discover. However, just because there isn't anything left to discover doesn't mean there isn't anything left to think about: as Aristotle argued, contemplation involves reflecting on and appreciating deep truths, rather than discovering those truths.[8] Accordingly, it doesn't look like gameplaying is the sole remaining victor for the ideal activity, as art, ethics, and contemplation—and probably many other activities—are left standing. Therefore, we can't conclude that gameplaying is the only or best thing to do in Utopia since other candidates remain a live option.

Nevertheless, even if gameplaying isn't the ideal of existence, it might still have unique attributes which set it apart from other Utopian activities. As Grasshopper's analysis demonstrates, if we examine the other likely candidates for Utopian activities (that is, those activities that are valuable in themselves), we see that, with the exception of gameplaying, they are all quite useful in non-Utopian situations—they all have instrumental value in addition to their intrinsic value.[9] For instance, scientific inquiry has intrinsic value in that it involves the excellent use of human capacities in the pursuit of something that itself has intrinsic value, namely knowledge. But it also has instrumental value in that the knowledge we acquire through science can be applied in various ways that improve our lives—science gave us great things like medicine and video games, after all. The practical use (and money-making potential) of science is so obvious and immediate to us that it often overwhelms our analysis of science's value, causing us to easily lose sight of its intrinsic value.

But this is not the case with gameplaying. As explained earlier, the achievements in gameplaying are not useful in the same way that achievements in science are. To see this, contrast the usefulness and efficiency of figuring out who murdered whom with what in Clue or getting pixelated gold coins in Mario with the discovery of electricity and its applications. The goals in games are not taken up for reasons other than those which pertain to the game. Once we stop playing Mario, we aren't concerned with pixelated gold coins, and if we weren't playing Clue but instead simply trying to answer a question whose solution is readily available, we would just open the envelope containing the answer rather than trying to figure it out. In contrast, the goals of science matter to us even when we stop doing science: when Edison completes his research on a practical way of using electricity for lighting, he is able to go home, turn on his incandescent lamp and enjoy the fruits of his labor in a way a Mario-player will never be able to enjoy their pixilated gold coins. Furthermore, if we could simply open an envelope and be told about all the mysteries of electricity and how to apply this knowledge without having to do centuries of research, it is hard to imagine a situation in which we wouldn't just open the envelope, even if we acknowledge that the activity of scientific research is valuable in itself.

Because the goals of games don't really matter outside of the game, the inherent value of gaming shines through. This idea is nicely captured by C. Thi Nguyen, whose work was discussed in Chapter 5, when he says, "In ordinary practical life, we pursue the means for the sake of the ends. But in striving play, we pursue the ends for the sake of the means. We take up a goal for the sake of the activity of struggling for it."[10] Gameplaying's value is unique in this respect.

PLAYING MAN BLUES

At this point, you may be thinking, "Hey, I like games a lot, but calling gaming the ideal of existence seems ludicrous." Even if we temper Grasshopper's claim to say that gaming is one among several other Utopian activities, you might still find yourself thinking that gaming does not belong amongst the set of activities that define a good life—that, perhaps, there is something missing from the gaming life. We noted above that the Utopian life sounds boring, and perhaps gameplaying would alleviate that boredom, but one might argue that a life of play still can't be a good life because such a life will be unsatisfying or unfulfilling. In fact, it might be the case that whole idea that Utopian life is work-free life is incoherent: if work is essential to a meaningful life, then Utopian life would involve work.

We can pick out two different reasons why one might think Grasshopper's version of Utopia lacks meaning, and unpacking them will help us better understand the inherent value of play and leisure. First, one might argue that in order for people to feel like they are living satisfying lives, they must always have something to strive for and achieve. As one of Grasshopper's disciples, Skepticus, points out, "[W]hen there are no more worlds to conquer we are filled not with satisfaction but despair."[11] Skepticus has in mind here Alexander the Great's insatiable desire to bring all countries under his domain, but we need look no further than the stereotypical mid-life crisis to see this objection in action: having achieved the traditional markers of a successful life—family, house, stable and well-paying career—it is common for adults to feel lost and melancholic even though they have everything they wanted. A similar predicament often faces retirees: while working, we may dream of the day when it's over, but upon retirement, life stagnates. If you are not yet at those life-stages, you have probably still felt the emptiness that follows achieving a big goal you have worked hard for (graduation, sports championship, etc.), and the pangs of nostalgia for the times—as frantic and stressful as they may have been—when you were absorbed in the process of attaining that goal. After working so hard, it's of course nice to take a break and relax for a bit (perhaps play some of your Steam library backlog), but the life of leisure gets old and eventually we feel the need to return to the grind (we feel antsy to return to the ant life, if you will).

Gaming gives us things to work for like attaining gold, defeating enemies, and saving princesses, but Skepticus' point seems to be not only that we yearn for things to strive for, but that we yearn for *real* and *meaningful* things to strive for: in order to feel satisfied and fulfilled, we need to feel useful and productive. Because the fruits of our gaming labors are useless, a life of play would leave us unfulfilled. Grasshopper, in his response to Skepticus, acknowledges that Skepticus is likely correct: the sad fact of the matter is that "[l]ife for most people will not be worth living if they cannot believe that they are doing *something* useful, whether it is providing for their families or formulating a theory of relativity."[12]

Grasshopper's response suggests that the seeming absurdity of his thesis that the Utopian life is the life of play stems, not from it being illogical, but rather from it being utterly foreign to our work-oriented lifestyle. Such is the tragic irony of our attitudes toward work and play. On the one hand, once the need for work is removed, we would be left with only the leisurely activities we choose for ourselves, a state of living we often fantasize about whilst in midst of working. On the other hand, Grasshopper recognizes that people find it very difficult to stop equating value solely with usefulness and productivity, and insofar as we think of things this way, we will never fully appreciate leisure and gameplaying. A life of play might feel dissatisfying until we can shift our focus away from instrumental value, but this does not mean that such a life must be unfulfilling and meaningless—perhaps we just need to change our attitudes to reflect the basic idea that a meaningful life is not necessarily the same thing as a productive life.

A second reason one might argue that a Utopian life cannot be a life of leisure has to do with the belief that a truly good life requires some amount of suffering. The basic idea is that, in order to grow as a person and truly appreciate life, one must experience hardship and work to overcome it. Such a belief is common throughout human thought. For example, the lotus flower is a Buddhist metaphor for the relationship between suffering and flourishing: just as the lotus requires nourishment from the messy unpleasant mud it grows in for its beautiful flower to blossom, so too do humans require messy and unpleasant experiences to reach their full potential.[13] A similar idea is also commonly expressed when considering the problem of evil in the Judeo-Christian tradition: if God is powerful enough to create the world in any way he wants, why would he include things like hurricanes and disease that cause humans so much suffering? One classic response to this worry is that God allows evil because the obstacles in life are opportunities for growth and the cultivation of virtue. Enduring and overcoming hardships builds character, so a life with evil is better than a life without.[14] A similar secular view is expressed in the movie *The Matrix*, when one of the "agents" describes how the first Matrix was designed to be a perfect world with no suffering, but no one accepted the program. The agent's theory is that it was rejected because "as a species, human beings define their reality through misery and suffering."[15] The idea is that our character is forged in the fires of life, and a life of leisure would lack the requisite trials and tribulations. Thus, the life of play would not be a meaningful life.

This objection to Grasshopper's Utopia presents a resoundingly bleak view of life, as it holds that we must endure suffering to be happy and fulfilled (not to mention how unfairly suffering is distributed among people). But, assuming that a good life does require some amount of *struggle*, Grasshopper's view of Utopia provides an account of flourishing that allows for struggle without *suffering*.[16] Gameplaying allows us to set obstacles and then strive to overcome them, so we can continuously improve ourselves and our skills in the context of the games. The gameplayers in Utopia can live meaningful lives, challenging themselves and growing in response, all without substantive suffering. It is a far more optimistic and, in our opinion, truthful view to maintain that we can flourish without hurricanes destroying towns and disease killing entire families.

WINTER IS COMING

We have shown that a Utopian life could consist of a life free from work, with only gameplaying to occupy our time. There is, of course, one glaring problem with this picture: we don't actually live in Utopia! Because "there *are*," as Prudence, one of Grasshopper's disciples, puts it, "winters to guard against," we can't sit around playing games all day.[17] In our current state, and the state we will be in for the foreseeable future, we must work to satisfy not only our basic needs, but also our obligations and commitments to others. In a world ridden with problems, it isn't unreasonable for people to wonder what role gameplaying should have in life. Perhaps it is selfish to put so much effort into saving pixelated princesses when there are real people suffering all around us, and when we do so, we are like children lounging on the couch while our parents do all the chores. Perhaps it is the case that in Utopia the life of the grasshopper is good, but in our non-Utopian reality, the good life requires us to be ants, working on solving the world's problems.

This criticism of play is similar to the one put forth by the 19th-century philosopher T. H. Green, who argued that when the conditions of life do not meet a sufficient threshold of well-being for all people, artistic activities cease to have actual value and it is wrong to pursue them. Under conditions in which a society's "civil life is crushed out and its moral energies debased. . .occupation with music might imply indifference to claims of the human soul which must be satisfied in order to the attainment of a life in which the value of music could be actualized."[18] At such points in history, art only has *potential* value for future societies living in more harmonious times. One might thus agree with Green and argue that, though play may be valuable in Utopian times, in our current era full of human suffering, we should be doing something better with our time. We should, perhaps, be living the life of the Purely Moral Ant, who completely dedicates their life to promoting the greater good. Moral goods are intrinsically valuable, so under non-Utopian conditions, one might argue the life of the Purely Moral Ant is the best life.

Although there is an element of truth to these objections, there are several problems with the view that we ought to pursue the life of the Purely Moral Ant. First, there is the practical issue that the Purely Moral Ant's life is simply too demanding for human beings to bear. A life spent tirelessly working toward improving society would be far too mentally and physically taxing on us. We would eventually burn out, and then be unable to do any work toward the good at all. Human beings need physical and mental breaks, and playing games can provide the requisite rest and leisure. Thus, if humans *were* to pursue the Moral Ant life, gameplaying could still have a role to play.[19] One might thus argue that a more realistic life for us to aspire to is the Feasibly Moral Ant life, in which we work toward the good most of the time but incorporate leisure time so that we can continue working. On such a view, play has a role in the good life in so far as it facilitates further moral work.

However, this way of thinking about the good life and the role of play within it has conceptual issues as well. It isn't clear that a life *completely* dedicated to others is a great life *for you*. If the ultimate end of your life is to promote the greatest good, then there is no real time for your personal projects and hobbies, except insofar as they provide the rest necessary for you to continue promoting the greatest good. But if you pursue your own personal interests, projects, and desires *only* so that you can help others more, then it becomes hard to see how this is *your* life. In such a life, the actual things that interest and fascinate you are held hostage to the needs of others. When we think of living a meaningful, good, and interesting life, *some* consideration needs to be afforded to our own interests, *even if* this comes at the cost of service to others.[20] Unless the world radically changes, there is always going to be some moral crises occurring, and it is unreasonable to say that activities like playing games lack intrinsic value until all crises are adverted.

To be clear, we aren't saying that you have no obligations to the environment or the greater good. We believe that living well requires the cultivation of virtue, and virtue extends to helping others, including the environment, more generally.[21] It is likely that most of us pay insufficient attention to the interests of others and think of our own self-interest too narrowly. However, it is also an error to not appreciate and enjoy the value of play for its own sake, independently of its service to some higher purpose. Helping others is important and is part of a life well-lived, but there are other excellences and goods that go beyond morality narrowly construed, such as artistic skill, knowledge, style, and humor. Gameplaying is one of these goods; indeed, play is seen as a fundamental human right. When we immerse ourselves in play, we express freedom, leisure, and enjoyment.[22]

Hence, there is a deep problem with endorsing the attitude of the Feasibly Moral Ant and identifying the value of play solely in terms of how it contributes to our moral development (or endorsing other permutations of Ant life that value play for its contribution to knowledge acquisition or productivity): it fundamentally blurs the work/play distinction and thereby blinds us from appreciating play itself.[23] John Tasioulas aptly notes that identifying the value of play in terms of achievement

> is a sophisticated manifestation of a problematic trend in modern life, one that has been aptly described as 'the invasion of play by the rhetoric of achievement.' As such,

it is a defense of games in the spirit of work ethic, and so yet another expression of the imperialist tendencies of the latter in our culture.[24]

Nonetheless, as mentioned above, there is an element of truth to the "winter is coming" objection. Whether we wanted them or not, we have various personal, social, and environmental obligations.[25] If improving our Kill Death Assists (KDA) ratio comes at the cost of the complete disregard of these obligations, then we are deviating from the path of virtue. But it is also an error to be incapable of taking time to stop to smell the roses (or destroy the enemy's base). Perhaps the best way to think about this is to follow Aristotle's thought that there is a virtue of play. The virtuous person avoids the deficiency of being a bore and the excess of being a buffoon and hits the sweet spot of playing in the right way, to the right degree, at the right time.[26] So, our response to the "winter is coming" objection is that, yes, in our non-Utopian condition, we must work jobs and help others, but we should also enjoy laughing with our friends while we shoot zombies. And strange as it may sound, when we do this, we are engaged in a fundamentally good activity that requires no further justification.

THE GREAT-SOULED GAMER

We've argued that play is intrinsically valuable and that there is a virtue of play that appreciates and exercises this value in the appropriate way and a vice of play that fails to do so. However, this is a book on video games, so you might be wondering whether *video gameplay* specifically is intrinsically valuable: after all, it could be the case that play *in general* is valuable, but some types of play are not. If hunting humans is your preferred game, you will not find a defense of its value here (or, we assume, anywhere)—some forms of play involve conditions that make them impermissible or irresponsible despite the overall value of play. Given that there are many forms of play and video games are associated with all kinds of negative things, one may argue that less controversial play should be pursued instead (to our knowledge, no one has accused *Candy Land* of causing mass shootings). But, assuming you haven't skipped the rest of the book to get here, you should now be aware that many of the criticisms against video games are misguided and video games do in fact have many positive attributes. Video gameplay is thus a fundamentally valuable activity.[27]

To be clear, though, we haven't argued that video game-playing is the *best* play activity, nor will we. When it comes to leisure activities, people must be free to choose what they personally want based on their own preferences and desires. In fact, to try and determine the *best* play activity would miss the entire point of what makes play valuable. Leisure, play, and amusement aren't about maximization and that is exactly what makes them relaxing and desirable activities: when we relax and play, the choice of activity is entirely up to us, and we make the choice that we do for the sole reason that we want to do that activity. Leisure time is a no-pressure, no-stakes affair, and once we start thinking about leisure time in terms of the best use of our time, the stakes have suddenly been raised and the pressure is on. Play and relaxation are pure expressions of our freedom, as the activities chosen are chosen without any external considerations, so one cannot play in the fullest sense—and certainly can't relax—if one is being compelled to do the activity out of some desire to maximize their potential or use their time wisely. Asking what play activity is best is thus antithetical to the very idea of leisure, as it would destroy the leisurely nature of the activity!

When it comes to leisure activities, a degree of autonomy needs to be allowed. That is, so long as the leisure activity isn't obviously negative and has some redeeming quality, it isn't bad that one pursues this activity *even if* other activities could be more beneficial. This means that to properly play and relax, one must consider what one enjoys and wants to do. It is unlikely to be the case, unless you are a strange being, that when it comes time to play and relax, the activity you always desire and enjoy is the activity that maximizes your potential. So, while video games might not be the optimal way to improve yourself, it misses the point of play and leisure to think that they need to be. If we are to appreciate the value of play for its own sake, and not as a way to be better ants, then we must not always look toward the potential benefits of the activity, but rather we should look at what activity we want to pursue. That is, assuming we want to be "great-souled and free."[28]

WHEN GAMING BECOMES WORK

We argued earlier that there is a virtue of play that involves having the appropriate attitude toward play. Playing too much or playing too little are obvious ways to fail to hit the mark of virtue, but there is a subtler way as well: treating gameplaying as work. To get a grasp of this phenomenon, let's turn to sound scientific evidence: Reddit. In a post labeled "Playing *Destiny* 2 now is the most boring thing i do," G01dberg writes:

> Seriously. It is more boring then my work. I only do bounties because i want some dust to spend in eververse. . . . I want to play other games but because of fomo [fear of missing out], i have to do this boring stuff. I suppose one day i will just drop the game and wont come back. Thanks bungie.[29]

Doranpls faced a similar quandary regarding "Old School *Runescape*":

> After I realized I was taking bathroom breaks at work so I could do a mundane/repetitive task to make money in the game (birdhouse runs), I seriously questioned why I was playing the game, when all the activities I was doing seemed like pointless, boring grinding.[30]

One of the things that surprises SM the most about her gaming friends is just how frequently they complain about the game they are playing—*whatever* game it happens to be. Take one recent exchange that occurred while the people in the voice channel were playing two different group-content games:

- Rage: Your group is suffering, our group is suffering.
- Asmo: Yeah dude, that's what video games are in 2023—suffering.
- Dem: I don't even know why I play games anymore.

Although this seemed like an opportunity for self-reflection, it wasn't: despite the allegedly torturous nature of the game, they went on to stay up all night grinding loot.

What is interesting about these scenarios is that they simultaneously express dislike of a game and an urge to play it. What is going on here? Why are we choosing to spend our limited free time on boring and painful games that are even less fun than our jobs? At least when we go to work, we are doing so because we want the outcome of the activity—a paycheck. But in the case of gaming, players are not even getting anything out of suffering through the game, other than rewards that can only be utilized in the game they allegedly dread!

What are we to make of this attitude toward play? Although we can't account for every player's idiosyncrasies, we think that in such cases there is often some aspect of the game that players find tedious or uninteresting, but they endure it for the sake of something else game-related that they find interesting. For example, one might suffer through tedious tasks to acquire gear that allows them to play in a new way or to attempt more challenging content, or one may complete a boring game just to see what happens. Such attitudes are not entirely unique to games—plenty of readers and movie watchers have endured a book or movie that has overstayed its welcome. And few activities are *entirely* enjoyable: part of becoming an adult involves accepting that if you want to ride a roller coaster, you will need to wait in line. In our non-Utopian world, fun activities coincide with some boringness; that's just the way it is.

However, what is perhaps unique to video games is that gamers will sometimes continue to play the game despite getting *no* enjoyment from it. Indeed, gamers will often "cheese" encounters (use glitches or game-design oversights) to defeat a challenge more easily. For instance, in *Destiny* 2's Last Wish raid, rather than doing elaborate game mechanics to bring about a damage phase on the boss Riven, players found that if you stood in the back wall, you could bypass the mechanics requirement and go straight to the damage phase. An occasional game exploit can save a great deal of time and boredom if the activity is lame and grindy, so it can make sense to cheese it for the loot.[31] However, some exploits detract from interesting mechanics, as is the case with Riven, so by cheesing an encounter, one potentially misses out on fun. And some players try to cheese the *entire* game. When this occurs, it is unclear the player is even playing the game since they are trying to avoid all of the gameplay mechanics, and just trying to get the loot.

To help make sense of what is going on here, we can distinguish the activity internal to gameplaying from the external benefits.[32] For instance, if you hate playing a video game but do so for money, you are not playing because you enjoy the internal activity of the game itself but simply for external benefits, namely money. However, the external benefits need not be tied to the "real world," as they could be in-game loot or cosmetics. In contrast, if you enjoy the game mechanics and challenges, then you are playing because you enjoy the internal activity of the game itself. Of course, it is possible to play for both reasons. A professional gamer, for example, might both love the game and choose to play it because of the financial rewards. People who dislike the game mechanics or structure, but enjoy getting the loot could be said to play the "Chasing Loot game," rather than the specific video game, because they enjoy the internal activity of chasing loot and not the specific video game in which they happen to play Chasing Loot.

This internal/external distinction can help one sort through one's reasons for playing a game, and by doing so, one can evaluate whether they are taking the proper attitude toward the game. If you are only playing a game for external benefits, then you are essentially treating the game as a means to acquire some good—be it money, reputation, or some shiny in-game trinket—which means you are treating the game as work. This is the wrong attitude to take toward play: if our hobbies become tedious activities we endure to get rewards, we are no longer playing. Instead, we are ants, sneaking work into play.

In the previous section, we argued that play requires a certain amount of autonomy. Accordingly, if you enjoy the

Chasing Loot game over the actual game, then it doesn't make sense to criticize your choice of game since it ought to be your choice, and the Chasing Loot game is a legitimate game.[33] However, as the Reddit posts make clear, many gamers don't actually enjoy playing the Chasing Loot game despite continuously doing so. When this happens, the activity ceases to be play and instead becomes work. And when this becomes a pattern, one misses out on the virtue of play and acquires one of its accompanying vices. As games become more "grindy" and lack a clear endpoint, it is important to be honest with yourself about why you are playing and what you enjoy. Play is a wonderful thing; accordingly, we mustn't lose sight of this and let play become work.

LIVING THE GOOD LIFE AS ASSHOPPERS

This chapter took a departure from the previous ones in its attempt to argue for the value of play itself, rather than focusing on how gaming can help one develop excellences like fortitude, creativity, and friendship, but we'll now bring the ideas together. Although *eudaimonia* requires some ant-like attitude of working to improve ourselves, it also requires some of Grasshopper's attitude toward play as well—to live the good life, we should combine the two and live as "asshoppers."[34]

To understand the harmony between gameplay and virtue, it will be helpful to draw upon the Stoic "dichotomy of control," which divides what is up to us from what is not.[35] The things that are *internal* to you—your beliefs, desires, and choices—are entirely *up to you*. The things that are *external* to you—like where you are born, how people around you behave, whether your dog accidentally poops on the carpet, and whether the restaurant has run out of the dish you wanted—are not under your control. Importantly, though, the way you react to the things outside your control very much is in your control: although it is not up to you whether the restaurant still has the "catch of the day" available, you can choose how you react to this news, whether it be with a public tantrum or a graceful acceptance that you will be having pasta instead. This means that no matter how bad the external circumstances appear, you can still find success and happiness by focusing on what you can control and excelling in that regard—happiness and success lie in your own hands. You may not have planned on getting the pasta, but by approaching the situation with calm acceptance, you can still find yourself having an enjoyable meal, while the person screaming over the lack of fish will have a miserable night. The actual outcome (whether you ate fish or pasta) doesn't really matter—all that matters is how you approached and handled the situation.

Now, those basic foundations of Stoic virtue theory are fairly easy to understand in the abstract, and you might acknowledge that focusing on the things you do not have control of is the cause of much unhappiness and dissatisfaction in life. However, it is quite difficult to take these lessons to heart and live accordingly. It is hard to distance ourselves from outcomes, as society all too often measures our success according to measurable outputs. Furthermore, it can be hard to *motivate* ourselves to put effort into activities because they are good in themselves, rather than because of the goods they bring about. We can recognize that doing philosophy is intrinsically valuable, but it is hard to imagine doing it in *complete* absence of other goods it brings about, like a good grade on a paper or appearing intelligent in conversation with others. Without these external motivators, we might find ourselves simply skimming or dozing off in our chairs instead. So how can we balance putting in the effort required to sincerely engage in virtuous activities, without caring too much about the external outcomes such activities might bring about?

This is where the attitudes we take up in gameplay matter. The Stoic philosopher Epictetus notes that expert gamers are indifferent to the materials that they are playing with, and instead care about making skilled plays with the material. Furthermore, in order to play a game well, gamers must divorce themselves from the outcome and focus instead on playing the game: "If we are afraid to throw the ball, or nervous about catching it, then the fun is lost; and how can we preserve our composure when we are uncertain about what next to do?"[36] Gamers and athletes alike often speak of the importance and enjoyment of being "in the zone"—the smooth flow of losing yourself in the moment, of moving and reacting with grace and skill—but this only occurs when we stop caring about the result. When players become too preoccupied with outcomes, they not only become prone to anxiety and fear, resulting in worse play, they also stop having fun playing.

By approaching life with the gamer's attitude, we can experience what the Stoics call the "smooth flow" of life, living happily, virtuously, and in harmony with the world around us.[37] The gamer's attitude recognizes that what matters is not the results of the game, but rather what one does while playing the game—indeed, the game is played so that they can do something interesting and fun. As Grasshopper teaches us in his analysis of Utopia, the fact that gaming is valuable despite its meaningless outcomes makes it unique amongst the other intrinsically valuable activities. When we choose to play, we are doing so *only* because the activity *itself* is good, and this is precisely what makes it not only valuable, but fun. Gaming as an activity thus allows us to practice how to live virtuously with the right attitude, working toward cultivating the right beliefs, desires, choices, and skills while maintaining the indifference toward outcome that allows us to enjoy ourselves along the way. The attitude we take up in gameplay is thus an attitude we should take up in the good life: a life well-lived is a life well-played.

KEY POINTS

- Suits argued that gameplaying is the central Utopian activity because, unlike other intrinsically valuable activities, it is entirely taken up for its own sake.
- While Suits' argument might not be entirely successful in ruling out other potential Utopian activities, it does demonstrate that gameplaying is a paradigmatic intrinsically valuable activity. Such a perspective provides a hopeful view of life since the value of gameplaying isn't tied to any need or defect—it, hence, points to the possibility of having a good life without suffering.
- One might worry that in our non-Utopian world, play cannot be valuable because we should spend our time working on bettering the world. However, living well requires we not only help others, but also pursue our own interests and hobbies, which can include gaming.
- While video games might not be the play activity that maximizes our personal development, play activities needn't be optimal. When it comes to leisure, a certain degree of autonomy needs to be allowed or else the activity would be work.

- Since play is a fundamental value, developing the right attitude toward play is a virtue and the wrong attitude a vice. Gamers should avoid the vices of gaming too much and of treating play as work. We treat play as work when we do in-game activities we despise for loot.

—GGs, SM and NB out.

Notes

INTRODUCTION

1. https://www.theesa.com/resource/2022-essential-facts-about-the-video-game-industry/;https://www.marketwatch.com/story/videogames-are-a-bigger-industry-than-sports-and-movies-combined-thanks-to-the-pandemic-11608654990;https://www.statista.com/statistics/246892/value-of-the-video-game-market-in-the-us/; see also Egenfeldt-Nielsen, Smith, and Tosca 2020, chs. 2, 9.

2. https://www.cnn.com/2021/08/31/tech/china-ban-video-games-minor-intl-hnk/index.html; https://www.scmp.com/tech/big-tech/article/3156540/china-vs-video-games-why-beijing-stopped-short-gaming-ban-keeping.

3. NE I.7.1098a18–19.

4. For examples of virtue in non-moral senses, see Republic 1.335b; Republic 1.353b–c; see also, Parry and Thorsrud 2021, sect. 1.

5. Politics 8.6.1341a20–21.

6. On this distinction, see Williams 1985; see also, Athanassoulis 2013, ch. 2. We use "ethics" to refer to the broader approach, and "morality" to refer to the narrow approach.

7. For defenses that virtue ethics is the best approach to gaming, see Bartel 2020, ch. 3; McCormick 2001; and Sicart 2009, ch. 2. Note that philosophers examine video games from a variety of perspectives: besides looking at the consequences and the character of the player, some take a Kantian or duty-based perspective (see Flattery 2021; LaBossiere 2017; Ryland 2019), others a feminist perspective (Chess 2017; Mikkola 2018; Patridge 2018), and many others (see Hayse 2023; Schulzke 2020; Young 2014).

8. There are many flavors of virtue theory. For instance, theories inspired by: ancient Eastern philosophy, such a Confucian virtue ethics (see Kim

2020); utilitarianism (see Driver 2001); Kantianism (Baxley 2010), and many more. Technically, ethicists today distinguish "virtue theory" from "virtue ethics": virtue theory is theory about what the virtues are and how to evaluate character, while virtue ethics is theory about right and wrong action (see Adams 2006, ch. 1). For the sake of simplicity, we set this distinction aside.

9. *Culture and Value* 14e.
10. *Voices of Wittgenstein* 33.
11. For discussions of what a video game is, see Egenfeldt-Nielsen, Smith, and Tosca 2020, ch. 3; Karhulahti 2015; Kriss 2020, 50–51. On different game types, see Wolf and Perron 2023, Part 2.
12. *Vatican Sayings* 52 (see LS 22F (5)).
13. https://catholichousehold.com/what-10-priests-say-video-games/.

1

1. https://www.nytimes.com/2018/03/08/business/video-games-violence.html; https://www.youtube.com/watch?v=y6FncsNES3s; https://www.movie-censorship.com/report.php?ID=3218.
2. https://www.nytimes.com/2019/08/05/sports/trump-violent-video-games-studies.html; https://www.huffpost.com/entry/maduro-spiderman-venezuela-violence_n_3949942.
3. Plato was concerned that media (poetry, tragedy, and comedy) with immoral content developed immoral citizens and that media that elicits irrational emotions leads to general irrationality; see *Republic* 2–3, 10. Aristotle, for his part, argued that experiencing emotions through art can provide therapy through catharsis; see *Poetics* 6.1449b22–28; *Politics* 8.7.1341b32–1342a17. In addition, Aristotle's general method for assessing art differed from his teachers. Rather than reducing the aesthetic quality to its educational and moral value like Plato, he assessed it by the standards of the type of art that it was.
4. Bandura, Ross, and Ross 1961.
5. Anderson 2000.
6. See Anderson and Bushman 2001; Lansford 2012.
7. Allen and Anderson 2017, 1–3.
8. American Psychological Association (2020), "APA Resolution on Violent Video Games." Accessed at https://www.apa.org/about/pol

icy/resolution-violent-video-games.pdf. However, it should be noted that the media division of the APA wrote an open letter response to this letter, see https://www.scribd.com/document/448927394/Division-46-Letter-to-the-APA-criticizing-it-s-recent-review-of-video-game-violence-literature.

9. However, it is possible that aggression could change for some other unrelated reason as well. So, in order to make sure that it is violent video games that caused the change in aggression, we also need to include what is known as a control group—a group that does some other, neutral task, like playing non-violent video games. By comparing the aggression between the violent games and non-violent games groups, experimenters are in a better position to claim that it is the violent video games specifically that cause an increase in aggression.

10. See Madigan 2016, 241–242.

11. See Madigan 2016, 243–245.

12. See Madigan 2016, 249; see also, Coulson and Ferguson 2016, 61–63; Drummond, Sauer, and Ferguson 2020.

13. See Markey and Ferguson 2017, ch. 3.

14. Ferguson, Copenhaver, and Markey 2020, 1428.

15. Ramos et al. (2013, 9) have argued that much of the research on video games and aggression may be an example of a circular argument, in which the conclusion that playing violent video games causes aggression was assumed to be true from the get-go, and then the research aimed to establish the truth of the claim.

16. Markey and Ferguson 2017, ch. 4.

17. Markey, Markey, and French 2015.

18. This is a central point of Schulzke 2020.

19. Our discussion of the psychological evidence of video games is by no means exhaustive, but it offers an overview of the claims and some general reasons to be skeptical. For other philosophical discussions of the evidence, see Bartel 2020, 61–68; Schulzke 2020, ch. 2; Tavinor 2009, ch. 8; Young 2014. For psychological discussions, see Bowman 2016; Coulson and Ferguson 2016; Hodent 2021, ch. 4; Kriss 2020, ch. 5; Madigan 2016, ch. 14; Markey and Ferguson 2017. For an overview, see Egenfeldt-Nielsen, Smith, Tosca 2020, ch. 9; Krapp 2023.

20. This idea is inspired from Tavinor 2009, ch. 8; see also, Bartel 2020, chs. 2 and 5. For the point that we need to go beyond negative

consequences, see Bartel 2020; Goerger 2017; McCormick 2001; Sicart 2009; Strain 2011; Young 2014. The topic discussed in this section relates to what Morgan Luck (2009) calls the "gamer's dilemma": virtual murder seems permissible, but virtual pedophilia doesn't, yet there doesn't seem to be a substantive difference between them— neither, for instance, causes direct physical harm. Thus, one must either abandon one of their intuitions or explain the relevant difference; see Ali 2015; Bartel 2020; Luck 2022; Patridge 2013; Young 2016.

21. Tavinor 2009, 171.

22. Madigan (2016, ch. 14) argues that one of the reasons violent games are appealing to many players is that they offer players a chance to experience competence, autonomy, and relatedness, which are core components of "self-determination theory."

2

1. The idea that athletics can improve character isn't new, but goes back to Plato (see *Republic* 2–3; *Laws* 7–8) and Aristotle (see *Politics* 8). For a discussion, see Reid 2012.

2. Chess was not always thought of positively: "Chess is a mere amusement of a very inferior character, which robs the mind of valuable time that might be devoted to nobler acquirements" (uncredited person, *Scientific American* July 2, 1859, 9; see Madigan 2016, 257).

3. No doubt that it applies to professional gaming, but since the focus of this book is on the recreational gamer, we will concentrate on that.

4. *Discourses* 2.5.18–20.

5. *Discourses* 2.5.21.

6. *Handbook* 4.

7. See NE 2.7.1108a24–27; 4.8. The Greek word *eutrapelia* is usually translated narrowly as "wittiness." For a broader interpretation, see Carli 2021; see also, Aquinas *Summa Theologica* 2.B.q.168.2 and Cicero, *On Duties* 1.103–104.

8. Madigan 2016, ch. 1.

9. *Republic* 2.359d–360d.

10. *Republic* 2.360d. For a discussion, see Baima and Paytas 2021, ch. 3.

11. NE 2.6.1106b30–34. Note that Aristotle thought that virtues were a "golden mean" between excess and deficiency (see NE 2.6); however,

such a view is not a feature of all ancient conceptions of virtue and is not without theoretical problems (see Hursthouse 2006), and thus we will not incorporate it.

12. *Meditations* 6.53.
13. The idea that a motive must be universalizable for it to be morally acceptable is developed by Kant; see the *Groundwork* 4:421; Korsgaard 1985.
14. The Greek virtue of moderation, or *sōphrosunē*, fits part of what we have in mind, since it includes good judgment, self-control, self-knowledge, and discipline. However, because we are using moderation in the narrow sense of self-control, we have chosen a different word.
15. *On Duties* 1.141.
16. Seneca, *On Anger* 1.2; Aristotle NE 4.5.
17. *Meditations* 6.6; next quote, 7.68.
18. See Suit's distinction between triflers, cheats, and spoilsports (2014, ch. 3); see also Wolf and Perron 2023, Part 4.
19. For a Stoic account on the injustice of lying and unknowingly saying falsehood, see *Meditations* 9.1.
20. *Meditations* 11.15.
21. Driver (2001) argues that ignorance is necessary for humility. We disagree: it is possible for an accomplished person to accurately assess their accomplishments and to speak humbly about them. In the grand scheme of things, no one's achievements are that significant.
22. On self-knowledge requiring the understanding of others, see Epictetus *Fragment* 1. For Socratic discussions of self-knowledge, see Plato *Charmides* 164e; *Protagoras* 343b; *Phaedrus* 229e; and *Philebus* 48c.
23. See Archterbosch, Milller, and Vamplew 2017 for a taxonomy of griefer types.
24. *Rhetoric* 2.7.1385a17–19.
25. *Meditations* 11.18.9.
26. On the leaky jar, see *Gorgias* 493b–494a; on scratching, see 494c–e.
27. For a discussion of the unity of the virtues, see Adams 2006, ch. 10.
28. See Adams 2006 for a discussion of virtue and context-sensitivity.

3

1. See Kowert 2016, 106–110 for information on social-psychological characteristics of gamers.

2. For the first point see, Cole and Griffiths 2007; on the second, see Williams et al. 2006. For a discussion of gaming, social activity, and "happiness," see McGonigal 2011.

3. See Kowert 2016, 98–101 for a summary of the displacement problem, along with a list of references for it.

4. Kowert 2016, 98. Note Kowert isn't defending this theory but is merely explaining it.

5. Another model combines both displacement and compensation, see Kowert 2016, 101–103.

6. See Domahidi, Festl, and Quandt, 2014, and for a philosophical discussion, see Søraker 2012.

7. The Greek word for friendship is *philia*, which includes the relationships we today consider friendships, but also can include parental, sibling, and communal relationships, which are not always considered friendships today.

8. NE 8.2.1155b27–1156a6.

9. NE 8.2–5. For a discussion of how friendships of use and pleasure can still involve good will and mutual affection, see Broadie 2002, 58–59; Cooper 1999, ch. 14; and Nussbaum 2001, 355–356.

10. On the dissolution of friendship and disputes, see NE 8.13–9.3.

11. *Discourses* 2.22.9; see also NE 8.4.

12. NE 9.12.1172a12–14.

13. NE 9.10.

14. NE 9.12.1172a1–8.

15. NE 9.9.1170b10–13.

16. NE 8.3.1156b17, 8.12.1161b28, 9.4.1166a31, 9.9.1170b7, 9.12.1171b1–1172a1.

17. NE 9.4.

18. NE 9.9.1170b12–14.

19. NE 9.9.

20. NE 8.5.1157b11–13.

21. On the distinction between communication and activity in MMORPGs, see Munn 2012. See also, Bülow and Felix 2014, 30–33; Vallor 2012, 196.

22. For Aristotle on friendship in family, see NE 8.12.

23. On thinking of virtue friendships as aspirational, see Cocking 2012.

24. See Cocking 2012.

25. See McFall 2012; Sharp 2012; and Vallor 2012.

26. See Cocking and Mathew 2000; Cocking, van den Hoven, and Timmermans 2012; Fröding and Peterson 2012; McFall 2012; Sharp 2012. For responses, see Bülow and Felix 2014; Elder 2018, ch. 8; Kaliarnta 2016; and Munn 2012.

27. The general ideas for this argument and the next are drawn from Bülow and Felix 2014, 25–29.

28. On this point, see Munn 2012.

29. McFall (2012, 229) argues, contra Munn 2012, virtue cannot be developed through online gaming.

30. This is similar to the Ring of Gyges scenario discussed in the previous chapter.

31. On this point, see Bülow and Felix 2014, 32; see also Søraker 2012.

32. See especially, Kriss 2020, ch. 4.

33. *Letters* 48.2–3.

4

1. Sometimes this is called "Gaming Disorder" (GD); for simplicity, we are treating GD and IGD as the same.

2. For an example of a person dying from excessive gaming, see https://www.cnn.com/2015/01/19/world/taiwan-gamer-death/index.html. For an example of gamers neglecting a toddler while raising a virtual baby, see https://www.theguardian.com/world/2010/mar/05/korean-girl-starved-online-game.

3. On the addiction debate, see https://www.nytimes.com/2019/10/22/magazine/can-you-really-be-addicted-to-video-games.html. Many objectors have banded together to write an opinion piece against gaming disorder, e.g., Van Rooij et al. 2018; see also Aarseth et al. 2017; Division 46 Committee 2018, https://div46amplifier.com/2018/06/21/an-official-division-46-statement-on-the-who-proposal-to-include-gaming-related-disorders-in-icd-11/.

4. Internet Gaming Disorder: https://www.psychiatry.org/patients-families/internet-gaming; see Radden 2023.

5. IGD diagnosis is based on the criteria of diagnosing addictions more generally, and so we can expect that if IGD becomes an official disorder, it will be grouped in the addiction category.

6. We say this a bit "tongue-in-cheek," as the DSM isn't intended for self-diagnosis.

7. See Starcevic 2017.

8. See King and Delfabbro 2016.

9. Petry et al. 2014, 1401, 1403.

10. https://gamequitters.com/cam/.

11. Szasz 1960. Note that this is our own interpretation of the phrase "problems in living," though it still captures Szasz's general idea. We are not endorsing Szasz's conclusions here. Instead, we are simply accepting Szasz's less controversial concern about over-medicalizing the struggles and challenges (and the ways we deal with them) that are simply part of normal human existence.

12. See, for example, Khantzian 1985.

13. Some psychologists have claimed that gaming might be a maladaptive coping mechanism, as it may be a way of avoiding problems rather than working toward solutions; see Schneider, King, and Delfabbro 2018. However, there has also been a push in the literature on coping mechanisms to move away from the maladaptive/adaptive dichotomy and instead focus on how individual subjects are using the coping mechanism in the specific context they find themselves in, rather than categorizing strategies themselves as good or bad; see Bonanno and Burton 2013.

14. Iacovides and Mekler 2019. On escapism and virtuality, see Silcox 2017; see also Chalmers 2022; Kissel and Ramirez 2024.

15. This connects to the "self-determination theory"; see Madigan 2016, ch. 14.

16. https://www.youtube.com/watch?v=HQvetA1P4Yg&t=1312s.

17. Iacovides and Mekler 2019, 7. For a discussion of the therapeutic benefits of gaming, see Bean 2021; Kriss 2020; Stone 2021.

18. King, Delfabbro, and Griffiths 2010.

19. B. F. Skinner popularized the basic "Skinner box" experimental setup and also performed some of the first work on reinforcement schedules; see Ferster and Skinner 1957. Skinner also noted early on the connection between variable rates of reinforcement in animals and casino gambling in humans; see Skinner 1953.

20. Griffiths 1993.

21. On FIFA, see https://www.bbc.co.uk/news/business-53337020. On gambling and loot boxes, see Griffiths 2021.

22. For an example of FOMO in gaming, see https://www.pcmag.com/opin
ions/the-limited-time-content-trap-fortnite-fomo-and-games-as-
a-service. On *Star Wars: Battlefront 2*, see https://www.businessinsider.
com/reddit-world-record-downvotes-ea-star-wars-battlefront-
2-2019-9.

23. APA quote: https://www.psychiatry.org/File%20Library/Psychiatrists/
Practice/DSM/APA_DSM-5-Internet-Gaming-Disorder.pdf; "brain on
drugs": https://nypost.com/2016/08/27/its-digital-heroin-how-scr
eens-turn-kids-into-psychotic-junkies/; and "heroin": https://www.
eurogamer.net/the-real-story-behind-the-suns-gaming-as-addictive-
as-heroin-headline.

24. Hodent 2021, 50.

25. For general overviews of the cognitive benefits of gaming, see Dale and
Green 2016; Hodent 2021, 46–48; Madigan 2016, ch. 15; Palaus et al.
2017. On the transfer of skill, see Bavelier et al. 2012. For a counter
perspective, see Sala, Tatlidil, and Gobet 2018.

26. Kriss 2020, 152–156.

5

1. One quick response to the manchild objection is that it is based on
an antiquated stereotype of gaming as only a male activity. However,
this response doesn't get to the heart of the objection, which is a
claim about value (see Chess 2017). Another quick response is that
the manchild objection is superficial: we agree that it is, but it is still
made in public forums and expressed to individuals (see Tavinor
2017, 99–102), and thus needs to be addressed.

2. Obviously, not everything that passes the "job interview test" will be
straightforwardly productive, such as jogging, camping, and reading
novels. That said, these activities indirectly translate into productivity
by showing characteristics such as discipline, adventurousness, and
intelligence. Furthermore, it is simply undeniable that we live in a
productive-oriented society.

3. For an overview of gamification, see Egenfeldt-Nielsen, Smith, and
Tosca 2020, ch. 8. For a critical analysis, see Nguyen 2020, ch. 9. For
a positive take, see McGonigal 2011.

4. *Gorgias* 485a–d.

5. However, Rubio did eventually change his position. https://www. insidehighered.com/quicktakes/2018/03/29/rubio-changes-tune-philosophers.
6. Aristotle, *Politics* 1.11.1259a16–18.
7. On the practical value of philosophy, see https://www.montclair.edu/ philosophy/2022/09/13/the-practical-value-of-studying-philosophy/.
8. *Republic* 7.514a–518b. Plato's allegory of the cave is related to Nozick's "experience machine." For a recent anthology on the philosophy of the experience machine and its connection to virtual worlds, see Silcox 2017; see also Chalmers 2022; Kissel and Ramirez 2024.
9. *Apology* 38a.
10. *Symposium* 205a; see also Aristotle, *NE* Book 1.
11. *Metaphysics* 1.1.980a21; *Arthur*, Season 3, Episode 11b.
12. Hitz 2021, 59.
13. For related objections to video games as art and responses, see Lopes 2010, chs. 2 and 7; see also Carroll 1998, chs. 1, 4, and 6 for a similar discussion with respect to "mass art."
14. "Triple fire emoji" https://twitter.com/mchammer/status/1365764 595667771392.
15. First quote: Hitz 2021, 94; second quote: 2012, 30.
16. See Hitz 2021, 30 and 93 for comparisons of gaming to pornography, drinking, and heroin; see also, Hitz 2021, 147.
17. See Schulzke 2020, ch. 4.
18. See Murdoch 1999, Part 1.
19. Schulzke 2020; see also, Hayse 2023.
20. Nussbaum 2001, 15.
21. Tavinor 2009, 143 (our italics).
22. Robson and Meskin 2016, 167. On make-believe, see Walton 1990, 209. On video games and narrative, see Egenfeldt-Nielsen, Smith, and Tosca 2020, ch. 7.
23. See Tavinor 2009, ch. 6.
24. In game studies, the "ludology–narratology debate" surrounds whether games should be viewed primarily through the lens of game-play or story (see Aarseth 2023; Arsenault 2023; Nguyen 2017; Tavinor 2009, ch. 2). For our purposes, all that matters is that both narrative-based games and non-narrative-based games can be objects of contemplation. Interestingly, in video games, the story and

gameplay can conflict with each other; see Tavinor 2009, ch. 6. This is just another interesting way video games can provoke thought.

25. Nguyen 2020, 17. Note that much of our discussion on agency is drawn from Nguyen 2020.
26. See Nguyen 2020, ch. 4.
27. See Nguyen 2020, ch. 5.
28. See Robson 2018.
29. See Meskin 2018. For an anthology on recent debates on the aesthetics of video games, see Robson and Tavinor 2018; see also Egenfeldt-Nielsen, Smith, and Tosca 2020, chs. 5 and 7; Wolf and Perron 2023, Part 3.

6

1. *Politics* 8.3.1338b2–4.
2. *Aesop's Fables*, Fable 156.
3. While Aristotle clearly defends leisure over productive work, he does dismiss amusement on the grounds that "it would be strange if the goal of life were amusement, and our lifelong efforts and sufferings aimed at amusing ourselves . . . but serious work and toil aimed at amusement appears stupid and excessively childish" (NE 10.6.1176b30–35). Plato's position on this issue is less clear; see D'Angour 2013.
4. Suits 2014, 9–10.
5. Suits 2014, 188–189.
6. On philosophy as the greatest activity, see Plato's *Republic* Books 5–7 and Aristotle, NE Book 10.6–8.
7. For the criticism of Suit's objections to art and morality, see Hurka 2014, xvi.
8. See NE 10.6–8; see also, NE 6; *Metaphysics* 1.1–2 and 12.
9. See Hurka 2014, xvii–xxii.
10. Nguyen 2020, 9.
11. Suits 2014, 189.
12. Suits 2014, 196.
13. See O'Hara 2014, 10.
14. See Hick 1978.
15. This idea is drawn from Ridge 2021b, 23–24; see also Schellenberg 1993, Part 2.

16. Ridge 2021b, 23–24.

17. Suits 2014, 10. For an introduction to the philosophy of games, see Nguyen 2017. For an introduction to the philosophy of games and play, see Ridge 2019; see also Ridge 2021b. For an introduction to games and play from a game studies perspective, see Egenfeldt-Nielsen, Smith, and Tosca 2020, ch. 3; Wolf and Perron 2023, Part 4; Embrick, Wright, and Lukacs 2012. On the reception of Suits in game studies, see Mitchell 2020. For a recent criticism of Suits, see Erspamer and Ridge 2021.

18. Green, *Prolegomena to Ethics*, sec. 381. For a discussion, see Hurka 1993, 165.

19. With respect to morality, see Railton 1984. There is also the issue that many contemporary moral problems are collective action problems, and thus it might not make sense to sacrifice significant fun in your life for a minor impact; see Johnson 2003; Raterman 2012; and Shahar 2016.

20. For arguments of this sort, see Athanassoulis 2013, chs. 1–2; Williams's objections in Smart and Williams 1973; and Wolf 1982. For a response, see Ashford 2000.

21. See Hill 1983.

22. On play as a fundamental good, see Tasioulas 2006.

23. See Oakeshott 2004, 313.

24. Tasioulas 2006, 251. He quotes from Lasch 1978, 65. On achievement, see Bradford 2015; Hurka 2014, xvii–xix; Tavinor 2017. On leisure and "slacking," see Suen 2021; see also Wright 2018.

25. All *Destiny* players will understand this reference.

26. See *NE* 2.7; 4.8, and our discussion in Ch. 2.

27. We are treating playing games as a form of play and play as a type of leisure activity. It might be the case that playing games and play are fundamentally distinct (see Suits 2014, app. 3; Ridge 2019); nevertheless, when we think about play as a fundamental human good, surely playing games fits in that category.

28. Aristotle, *Politics* 8.3.1338b2–4. Also, to be clear, though play involves leisure and relaxation, this doesn't mean that it is incompatible with striving and competition, as these can be what make play fun and interesting; see Juul 2013.

29. https://www.reddit.com/r/DestinyTheGame/comments/g5w3mr/
    playing_destiny_2_now_is_in_the_most_boring_thing/.
30. https://www.reddit.com/r/Games/comments/c25gx7/grinding_
    in_games_and_wondering_why_youre_even/.
31. The permissibility of cheesing encounters depends upon the terms of
    service and how it affects other players. If it doesn't affect other play-
    ers and doesn't violate any terms of service, then it is clearly permis-
    sible. However, if it does affect other players and does violate terms of
    service, then the issue is more complex.
32. For a related, and more nuanced, discussion, see Nguyen 2020, ch. 2.
33. Though see Nguyen 2020, ch. 6. For a discussion on video games and
    work infecting play under capitalism, see Wright 2018.
34. This portmanteau found in Suits 2014, 10.
35. See Irvine 2009 ch. 5; Epictetus *Discourses* 1.1; *Handbook* 1.
36. *Discourses* 2.5.17.
37. See LS 63c. On Stoic value and games, see Klein 2014; Ridge 2021a.

References

OLDER SOURCES

Aesop. 2003. *Aesop's Fables*. V. Jones (trans.). Barnes & Noble.

Aquinas. 1920. *Summa Theologiae*. 2nd edition. Literally Translated by Fathers of the English Dominican Province, Online Edition 2017 edited by K. Knight. https://www.newadvent.org/summa/.

Aristotle. 2019. *Nicomachean Ethics* [NE]. T. Irwin (trans.). 3rd edition. Hackett Publishing.

Aristotle. 1984. *The Complete Works: The Revised Oxford Translation*. 2 Volumes. J. Barnes (ed.). Princeton University Press.

Cicero. 1991. *On Duties*. M. T. Griffin and E. M. Atkins (eds. and trans.). Cambridge University Press.

Epictetus. 2008. *Discourses and Selected Writings*. R. Dobbin (ed. and trans.). Penguin Publishing.

Green, T. H. 1906. *Prolegomena to Ethics*. 5th edition. A. C. Bradley (ed.). Oxford University Press.

Homer. 2013. *The Odyssey*. S. Mitchell (trans.). Atria Books.

Kant, I. 2002. *Groundwork for the Metaphysics of Morals*. T. Hill Jr. and A. Zweig (trans.). Oxford University Press.

Long, A. A. and D. N. Sedley [LS]. 1987. *The Hellenistic Philosophers*. Volume 1 Translations of the Principal Sources, with Philosophical Commentary. Cambridge University Press.

Marcus Aurelius. 2002. *Meditations*. G. Hays (trans.). Modern Library Paperback.

Plato. 1997. *Plato's Complete Works*. J. Cooper and D. S. Hutchinson (eds.). Hackett Publishing.

Seneca. 2010. *On Anger*. R. A. Kaster (trans.). University of Chicago Press.

——. 2015. *Letters on Ethics*. M. Graver and A. A. Long (trans.). University of Chicago Press.

Wittgenstein, L. 1980. *Culture and Value: A Selection from the Posthumous Remains*. G. H. von Wright and H. Nyman (eds.) and P. Winch (trans.). Oxford.
——. 2003. *The Voices of Wittgenstein: The Vienna Circle*. G. Baker et al. (trans.). Routledge.

CONTEMPORARY SOURCES

Aarseth, E. 2023. "Ludology." In *The Routledge Companion to Video Game Studies*. M. Wolf and B. Perron (eds.), 255–259. Routledge

Aarseth, E., et al. 2017. "Scholar's Open Debate Paper on the World Health Organization ICD-11 Gaming Disorder Proposal." *Journal of Behavioral Addictions* 6: 267–270.

Adams, R. M. 2006. *A Theory of Virtue: Excellence in Being for the Good*. Oxford University Press.

Ali, R. 2015. "A New Solution to the Gamer's Dilemma." *Ethics and Information Technology* 17: 267–274.

Allen, J. J. and Anderson, C. A. 2017. "Aggression and Violence: Definitions and Distinctions." In *The Wiley Handbook of Violence and Aggression*. P. Sturmey (ed.), 1–14. Wiley-Blackwell Publishing. https://doi.org/10.1002/9781119057574.whbva001.

Anderson, C. 2000. "Violent Video Games Increase Aggression and Violence: Senate Commerce Committee Hearing on the Impact of Interactive Violence on Children." Tuesday, March 21, 2000" Retrieved 5/5/2023 from http://www.craiganderson.org/wp-content/uploads/caa/abstracts/2000-2004/00Senate.html.

Anderson, C. and Bushman, B. J. 2001. "Effects of Violent Video Games on Aggressive Behavior, Aggressive Cognition, Aggressive Affect, Physiological Arousal, and Prosocial Behavior: A Meta-Analytic Review of the Scientific Literature." *Psychological Science* 12: 353–359.

Archterbosch, L., Milller, C., and Vamplew, P. 2017. "A Taxonomy of Griefer Type by Motivation in Massively Multiplayer Online Role-Playing Games." *Behaviour & Information Technology* 36: 846–860.

Arsenault, D. 2023. "Narratology." In *The Routledge Companion to Video Game Studies*. M. Wolf and B. Perron (eds.), 588–596. Routledge.

Ashford, E. 2000. "Utilitarianism, Integrity, and Partiality." *Journal of Philosophy* 97: 421–439.

Athanassoulis, N. 2013. *Virtue Ethics*. Bloomsbury.

Baima, N. R. and Paytas, T. 2021. *Plato's Pragmatism: Rethinking the Relationship Between Ethics and Epistemology*. Routledge.

Bandura, A., Ross, D., and Ross, S. A. 1961. "Transmission of Aggression through the Imitation of Aggressive Models. *Journal of Abnormal and Social Psychology* 63: 575–582.

Bartel. C. 2020. *Video Games, Violence, and the Ethics of Fantasy*. Bloomsbury Press.

Bavelier, D., et al. 2012. "Brain Plasticity through the Life Span: Learning to Learn and Action Video Games." *Annual Review of Neuroscience* 35: 391–416.

Baxley. A. M. 2010. *Kant's Theory of Virtue: The Value of Autocracy*. Cambridge University Press.

Bean, A. 2021. "Therapeutic Use of Video Games." In *The Video Game Debate 2: Revisiting the Physical, Social, and Psychological Effects of Video Games*. R. Kowert and T. Quandt (eds.), 81–94. Routledge.

Bonanno, G. A. and Burton, C. L. 2013. "Regulatory Flexibility: An Individual Differences Perspective on Coping and Emotion Regulation." *Perspectives on Psychological Science* 8: 591–612.

Bowman, N. 2016. "The Rise (and Refinement) of Moral Panic." In *The Video Game Debate: Revisiting the Physical, Social, and Psychological Effects of Video Games*. R. Kowert and T. Quandt (eds.), 22–38. Routledge.

Bradford, G. 2015. *Achievement*. Oxford University Press.

Broadie, S. 2002. Philosophical Introduction, Commentary. In *Aristotle: Nicomachean Ethics*. S. Brodie and C. Rowe (eds.), 9–91, 261–452. Oxford University Press.

Bülow, W. and Felix, C. 2014. "On Friendship between Online Equals." *Philosophy and Technology*. 29: 21–32.

Carli, S. 2021. "Play a little! Aristotle on *Eutrapelia*." *Review of Metaphysics* 4: 465–495.

Carrol, N. 1998. *A Philosophy of Mass Art*. Oxford University Press.

Chalmers, D. J. 2022. *Reality+: Virtual Worlds and the Problems of Philosophy*. W. W. Norton & Company.

Chess, S. 2017. *Ready Player Two: Women Gamers and Designed Identity*. University of Minnesota Press.

Cocking, D. (ed.). 2012. *Ethics and Information Technology: Special Issue on Friendship Online* 14: 179–239.

Cocking, D. and Mathew, S. 2000. "Unreal Friends." *Ethics and Information Technology* 2: 223–231.

Cocking, D, van den Hoven, J., and Timmermans, J. 2012. "Introduction: One Thousand Friends." *Ethics and Information Technology* 14: 179–184.

Cole, H. and Griffiths, M. D. 2007. "Social Interactions in Massively Multiplayer Online Role-Playing Games." *CyberPsychology & Behavior* 10: 575–583.

Cooper, J. 1999. *Reason and Emotion: Essays on Ancient Moral Psychology and Ethical Theory*. Princeton University Press.

Coulson, M. and Ferguson, C. J. 2016. "The Influence of Digital Games on Aggression and Violent Crime." In *The Video Game Debate: Unravelling the Physical, Social and Psychological Effects of Digital Games*. R. Kowert and T. Quandt (eds.), 54–73. Routledge.

Dale, G. and Green, S. C. 2016. "Video Games and Cognitive performances." In *The Video Game Debate: Unravelling the Physical, Social and Psychological Effects of Digital Games*. R. Kowert and T. Quandt (eds.), 131–152. Routledge.

D'Angour, A. 2013. "Plato and Play: Taking Education Seriously in Ancient Greece." *American Journal of Play* 5: 293–307.

Domahidi, E., Festl, R., and Quandt, T. 2014. "To Dwell among Gamers: Investigating the Relationship between Social Online Game Use and Gaming-Related Friendships." *Computers in Human Behavior* 35: 107–115.

Driver, J. 2001. *Uneasy Virtue*. Cambridge University Press.

Drummond, A., Sauer, J, and Ferguson, C. J. 2020. "Do Longitudinal Studies Support Long-Term Relationships between Aggressive Game Play and Youth Aggressive Behaviour? A Meta-Analytic Examination." *Royal Society Open Science* 7: 2003737, https://royalsocietypublishing.org/doi/10.1098/rsos.200373.

Egenfeldt-Nielsen, S., Smith, J. H., and Tosca, S. P. 2020. *Understanding Video Games: The Essential Introduction*. 4th edition. Routledge.

Elder, A. M. 2018. *Friendship, Robots, and Social Media: False Friends and Second Selves*. Routledge.

Embrick, D. G., Wright, J. T., and Lukacs, A. (eds.). 2012. *Social Exclusion, Power, and Video Game: New Research in Digital Media and Technology*. Lexington Books.

Erspamer, M. and Ridge, M. 2021. "Are There Really Games in Utopia? A Reinterpretation of Suits' *The Grasshopper*. *Analysis* 81: 405–410.

Ferguson, C. J., Copenhaver, A. and Markey, P. 2020. "Reexamining the Findings of the American Psychological Association's 2015 Task Force on Violent Media: A Meta-Analysis." *Perspectives on Psychological Science* 15: 1423–1443.

Ferster, C. B and Skinner, B. F. 1957. *Schedules of Reinforcement*. Prentice-Hall.

Flattery, T. 2021. "May Kantians Commit Virtual Killings That Affect No Other Persons?" *Ethics and Information Technology* 22: 751–762.

Fröding, G. and Peterson, M. 2012. *Ethics and Information Technology* 14: 201–207.

Goerger, M. 2017. "Value, Violence, and the Ethics of Gaming." *Ethics and Information Technology* 19: 95–107.

Griffiths, M. D. 1993. "Fruit Machine Gambling: The Importance of Structural Characteristics." *Journal of Gambling Studies* 9: 101–120.

———. 2021. "A Brief Overview of Loot Boxes in Video Gaming." In *The Video Game Debate 2: Revisiting the Physical, Social, and Psychological Effects of Video Games*. R. Kowert and T. Quandt (eds.), 7–18. Routledge.

Hayse, M. 2023. "Ethics." In *The Routledge Companion to Video Games Studies*. M. Wolf and B. Perron (eds.), 597–587. Routledge.

Hick, J. 1978. *Evil and the God of Love*. 2nd ed. Harper & Row.

Hill, T. H. 1983. "Ideals of Human Excellence and Preserving Natural Environments." *Environmental Ethics* 5: 211–224.

Hitz, Z. 2021. *Lost in Thought: The Hidden Pleasures of an Intellectual Life*. Princeton University Press.

Hodent, C. 2021. *The Psychology of Video Games*. Routledge.

Hurka, T. 1993. *Perfectionism*. Oxford University Press.

———. 2014. "Introduction." In B. Suits, *The Grasshopper: Games, Life and Utopia*, ix–xxiii. 3rd ed. Broadview Press

Hursthouse, R. 2006. "The Central Doctrine of the Mean." In *The Blackwell Guide to Aristotle's Nicomachean Ethics*. R. Kraut (ed.), 96–115. Blackwell.

Iacovides, I. and Mekler, E. D. 2019. "The Role of Gaming during Difficult Life Experiences." In *CHI 2019: Proceedings of the 2019 CHI Conference on Human Factors in Computing Systems*. May 2019. Paper No. 223. https://doi.org/10.1145/3290605.3300453.

Irvine, W. B. 2009. *A Guide to the Good Life: The Ancient Art of Stoic Joy*. Oxford University Press.

Johnson, B. L. 2003. "Ethical Obligations in a Tragedy of the Commons." *Environmental Values* 12: 271–287.

Juul, J. 2013. *The Art of Failure: An Essay on the Pain of Playing Video Games*. MIT Press.

Kaliarnta, S. 2016. "Using Aristotle's Theory of Friendship to Classify Online Friendship: A Critical Counterview." *Ethics and Information Technology* 18: 65–79.

Karhulahti, V.-M. 2015. "Defining the Videogame." *Game Studies* 15. https://gamestudies.org/1502/articles/karhulahti https://gamestudies.org/1502/articles/karhulahti.

Khantzian, E. J. 1985. "The Self-Medication Hypothesis of Addictive Disorders: Focus on Heroin and Cocaine Dependence." *American Journal of Psychiatry* 142: 1259–1264.

Kim, R. 2020. *Confucianism and the Philosophy of Well-Being*. Routledge.

King, D. L. and Delfabbro, P. H. 2016. "The Cognitive Psychopathology of Internet Gaming Disorder in Adolescence." *Journal Child Psychology* 44: 1635–145.

King, D. L., Delfabbro, P. H., and Griffiths, M. D. 2010 "Video Game Structural Characteristics: A New Psychological Taxonomy." *International Journal of Mental Health and Addiction* 8: 90–106.

Kissel, A. and Ramirez, E. J. (eds.). 2024. *Exploring Extended Realities: Metaphysics, Psychological, and Ethical Challenges*. Routledge.

Klein, J. 2014. "Of Archery and Virtue: Ancient and Modern Conceptions of Virtue." *Philosophers' Imprint* 14 (19). http://hdl.handle.net/2027/spo.3521354.0014.019.

Korsgaard, C. 1985. "Kant's Formula of Universal Law." *Pacific Philosophical Quarterly* 66: 24–47.

Kowert. R. 2016. "Social Outcomes: Online Game Play, Social Currency, and Social Ability." In *The Video Game Debate: Unravelling the Physical, Social and Psychological Effects of Digital Games*. R. Kowert and T. Quandt (eds.), 94–115. Routledge.

Kowert, R. and Quandt, T. (eds.). 2016. *The Video Game Debate: Unravelling the Physical, Social and Psychological Effects of Digital Games*. Routledge.

———. 2021. *The Video Game Debate 2: Revisiting the Physical, Social, and Psychological Effects of Video Games*. Routledge.

Krapp, P. 2023. "Violence." In *The Routledge Companion to Video Game Studies*. M. Wolf and B. Perron (eds.), 432–438. Routledge.

Kriss, A. 2020. *The Gaming Mind: A New Psychology of Videogames and the Power of Play*. The Experiment.

LaBossiere, M. 2017. "Digital Tears Fell from Her Virtual Eyes: Or, the Ethics of Virtual Beings." In *Experience Machines: The Philosophy of Virtual Worlds*. M. Silcox (ed.), 169–182. Rowman & Littlefield.

Lansford, J. E. 2012. Aggression: Revisiting Bandura's Bobo Doll Studies. In *Developmental Psychology: Revisiting the Classic Studies*. A. M. Slater and P. C. Quinn (eds.), 176–190. Sage Publications.

Lasch, C. 1978. *The Culture of Narcissism: American Life in an Age of Diminishing Expectations.* W. W. Norton.

Lopes, D. M. 2010. *A Philosophy of Computer Art.* Routledge.

Luck, M. 2009. "The Gamer's Dilemma: An Analysis of the Argument's from the Moral Distinction between Virtual Murder and Virtual Paedophilia." *Ethics and Information Technology* 11: 31–36.

——. 2022. "The Grave Resolution to the Gamer's Dilemma: An Argument for a Moral Distinction between Virtual Murder and Virtual Child Molestation." *Philosophia* 50: 1287–1308.

Madigan, J. 2016. *Getting Gamers: The Psychology of Video Games and Their Impact on the People Who Play Them.* Rowman & Littlefield.

Markey, P. M. and Ferguson, C. J. 2017. *Moral Combat: Why the War on Violent Video Games Is Wrong.* BenBella Books.

Markey, P. M., Markey, C. N. and French, J. E. (2015). "Violent Video Games and Real-World Violence: Rhetoric versus Data." *Psychology of Popular Media Culture* 4: 277–295. https://psycnet.apa.org/doi/10.1037/ppm0000030.

McCormick. M. 2001. "Is it Wrong to Play Violent Video Games?" *Ethics and Information Technology* 3: 277–287.

McFall, M. T. 2012. "Real Character-Friends: Aristotelian Friendship, Living Together, and Technology." *Ethics and Information Technology* 14: 221–230.

McGonigal, J. 2011. *Reality is Broken: Why Games Make Us Better and How They Can Change the World.* Random House.

Meskin, A. 2018. "Videogames and Creativity." In *The Aesthetics of Video Games.* J. Robson and G. Tavinor (eds.), 95–111. Routledge.

Mikkola, M. 2018. In *The Aesthetics of Video Games.* "Pornography Videogames: A Feminist Examination." In J. Robson and G. Tavinor (eds.), 212–227. Routledge

Mitchell, L. 2020. "Reconsidering The Grasshopper: On the Reception of Bernard Suits in Game Studies." *Game Studies* 20. https://gamestudies.org/2003/articles/mitchell_liam.

Munn, N. J. 2012. "The Reality of Friendship within Immersive Virtual Worlds. *Ethics and Information Technology* 14: 1–10.

Murdoch, I. 1999. *Existentialists and Mystics: Writings on Philosophy and Literature.* Penguin.

Nguyen, C. T. 2017. "Philosophy of Games." *Philosophy Compass.* https://doi.org/10.1111/phc3.12426.

——. 2020. *Games: Agency as Art*. Oxford University Press.

Nussbaum, M. 2001. *The Fragility of Goodness: Luck and Ethics in Greek Tragedy and Philosophy*. Updated Edition. Cambridge University Press.

Oakeshott, M. *What is History? and Other Essays*. L. O'Sullivan (ed.). Imprint Academic.

O'Hara, P. E. 2014. *Most intimate: A Zen Approach to Life's Challenges*. Shambhala.

Palaus, M., et al. 2017. "Neural Basis of Video Gaming: A Systematic Review." *Frontiers in Human Neuroscience* 11. https://doi.org/10.3389/fnhum.2017. 00248.

Parry, R. and Thorsrud, H. 2021. "Ancient Ethical Theory." In *Stanford Encyclopedia of Philosophy*. E. N. Zalta (ed.). https://plato.stanford.edu/archives/fall2021/ entries/ethics-ancient/.

Patridge, S. 2013. "Pornography, Ethics, and Video Games." *Ethics and Information Technology* 15: 25–34.

——. 2018. "Videogames and Gendered Invisibility." In *The Aesthetics of Video Games*. J. Robson and G. Tavinor (eds.), 161–180. Routledge

Petry, N. M., et al. 2014. "An International Consensus for Assessing Internet Gaming Disorder Using the New DSM-5 Approach." *Addiction* 109: 1399–1406.

Radden, J. 2023. "Mental Disorder (Illness)." In *Stanford Encyclopedia of Philosophy*. E. N. Zalta & U. Nodelman (eds.). https://plato.stanford.edu/archives/ fall2023/entries/mental-disorder/.

Railton, P. 1984. "Alienation, Consequentialism, and the Demands of Morality." *Philosophy and Public Affairs* 13: 134–171.

Ramos, A., et al. 2013. *The Legal Status of Video Games: Comparative Analysis in National Approaches*. World Intellectual Property Organization.

Raterman, T. 2012. "Bearing the Weight of the World: On the Extent of an Individual's Environmental Responsibility." *Environmental Values* 21: 417–436.

Reid, H. 2012. *Athletics and Philosophy in the Ancient World*. Routledge.

Ridge, M. 2019. "Play and Games: An Opinionated Introduction." *Philosophy Compass*. DOI: 10.1111/phc3.12573.

——. 2021a. "Illusory Attitudes and the Playful Stoic." *Philosophical Studies* 178: 2965–2990.

——. 2021b. "Games and the Good Life." *Journal of Ethics and Social Philosophy* 19: 1–26.

Robson, J. 2018. "The Beautiful Gamer? On the Aesthetics of Videogame Performances." In *The Aesthetics of Video Games*. J. Robson and G. Tavinor (eds.), 78–94. Routledge.

Robson, J. and Meskin, A. 2016. "Video Games as Self-Involving Interactive Fictions." *The Journal of Aesthetics and Art Criticism* 74: 165–177.

Robson, J. and Tavinor, G. (eds.). 2018. *The Aesthetics of Video Games*. Routledge.

Ryland, H. 2019. "Getting Away with Murder: Why Virtual Murder in MMORPGs Can be Wrong on Kantian Grounds." *Ethics and Information Technology* 21: 105–115.

Sala, G, Tatlidil, K. S., and Gobet, F. 2018. "Video Game Training Does Not Enhance Cognitive Ability: A Comprehensive Meta-Analytic Investigation." *Psychological Bulletin* 144: 111–139.

Schellenberg, J. L. 1993. *Divine Hiddenness and Human Reason*. Cornell University Press.

Schneider, L. A., King, D. L and Delfabbro, P. H. 2018. "Maladaptive Coping Styles in Adolescents with Internet Gaming Disorder Symptoms." *International Journal of Mental Health and Addiction* 16: 905–916.

Schulzke, M. 2020. *Simulating Good and Evil: The Morality and Politics of Videogames*. Rutgers University Press.

Shahar, D. 2016. "Treading Lightly on the Climate in a Problem-Ridden World." *Ethics, Policy & Environment* 19: 183–195.

Sharp, R. 2012. "The Obstacles against Reaching the Highest Level of Aristotelian Friendship Online." *Ethics and Information Technology* 14: 231–239.

Sicart, M. 2009. *The Ethics of Computer Games*. MIT Press.

Silcox, M. (ed.). 2017. *Experience Machines: The Philosophy of Virtual Worlds*. Rowman & Littlefield.

Skinner, B. F. 1953. *Science and Human Behavior*. Macmillan.

Smart, J. J. C. and Williams, B. 1973. *Utilitarianism: For and Against*. Cambridge University Press.

Søraker, J. H. 2012. "Virtual Worlds and Their Challenge to Philosophy: Understanding the 'Intravirtual' and the 'Extravirtual.'" *Metaphilosophy* 43: 499–512.

Starcevic, V. 2017. "Internet Gaming Disorder: Inadequate Diagnostic Criteria Wrapped in a Constraining Conceptual Model: Commentary on: 'Chaos and confusion in DSM-5 Diagnosis of Internet Gaming Disorder: Issues, Concerns, and Recommendations for Clarity in the Field' (Kuss et al.)." *Journal of Behavioral Addiction* 6: 110–113.

Stone, J. 2021. "Extended Reality Therapy: The Use of Virtual, Augmented, and Mixed Reality in Mental Health Treatment." In *The Video Game Debate 2: Revisiting the Physical, Social, and Psychological Effects of Video Games*. R. Kowert and T. Quandt (eds.), 95–106. Routledge.

Strain, C. 2011. *Reload: Rethinking Violence in American Life*. Vanderbilt University Press.

Suen, A. 2021. *Why It's OK to Be a Slacker*. Routledge.

Suits, B. 2014. *The Grasshopper: Games, Life and Utopia*. 3rd ed. Broadview Press.

Szasz, T. S. 1960. *The Myth of Mental Illness. American Psychologists* 15: 113–118.

Tasioulas, J. 2006 "Games and the Good." *Aristotelian Society Supplementary Volume* 80: 237–264.

Tavinor, G. 2009. *The Art of Videogames*. Wiley-Blackwell Publishing.

——. 2017. "Welcome to the Achievement Machine: Or, How to Value and Enjoy Pointless Things. In *Experience Machines: The Philosophy of Virtual Worlds*. M. Silcox (ed.), 99–112. Rowman & Littlefield.

Vallor, S. 2012. "Flourishing on Facebook: Virtue Friendship & New Social Media." *Ethics and Information Technology* 14: 185–199.

Van Rooij, A. J., et al. 2018. "A Weak Scientific Basis for Gaming Disorder: Let Us Err on the Side of Caution." *Journal of Behavioral Addictions.* 7: 1–9.

Walton, K. 1990. *Mimesis as Make-Believe: On the Foundations of the Representational Arts*. Harvard University Press.

Williams, B. 1985. *Ethics and the Limits of Philosophy*. Harvard University Press.

Williams, D., et al. 2006. "From Tree House to Barracks: The Social Life of Guilds in World of Warcraft." *Games and Culture* 1: 338–361.

Wolf, M and Perron, B. (eds.). 2023. *The Routledge Companion to Video Game Studies*. Routledge.

Wolf, S. 1982. "Moral Saints." *Journal of Philosophy* 79: 419–439.

Wright, J. T. 2018. "Liberating Human Expression: Work and Play or Work versus Play." *American Journal of Play* 11: 3–25.

Young, G. 2014. *Ethics in the Virtual World: The Morality and Psychology of Gaming*. Routledge.

——. 2016. *Resolving the Gamer's Dilemma: Examining the Moral and Psychological Difference between Virtual Murder and Virtual Paedophilia*. Palgrave Macmillan.

Index

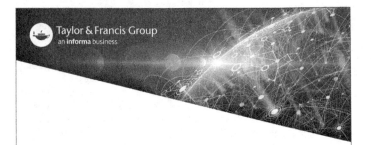

Taylor & Francis eBooks

www.taylorfrancis.com

A single destination for eBooks from Taylor & Francis
with increased functionality and an improved user
experience to meet the needs of our customers.

90,000+ eBooks of award-winning academic content in
Humanities, Social Science, Science, Technology, Engineering,
and Medical written by a global network of editors and authors.

TAYLOR & FRANCIS EBOOKS OFFERS:

A streamlined
experience for
our library
customers

A single point
of discovery
for all of our
eBook content

Improved
search and
discovery of
content at both
book and
chapter level

REQUEST A FREE TRIAL
support@taylorfrancis.com

Printed in the United States
by Baker & Taylor Publisher Services